CAMBRIDGE LIBRARY COLLECTION

Books of enduring scholarly value

History

The books reissued in this series include accounts of historical events and movements by eye-witnesses and contemporaries, as well as landmark studies that assembled significant source materials or developed new historiographical methods. The series includes work in social, political and military history on a wide range of periods and regions, giving modern scholars ready access to influential publications of the past.

Steel's Naval Remembrancer

David Steel was one of the most respected and prolific naval publishers of the early nineteenth century. His published volumes focused on naval strategy and shipbuilding techniques, and he was the first to publish regular Navy Lists. This volume, first published in 1801, contains information concerning British naval battles and losses which occurred during the early part of the French Revolutionary Wars, 1793–1800. This volume lists all ships belonging to the major European powers involved in the war which had been destroyed, describes settlements and colonies which had been captured by the British Navy, lists ships with details concerning their crew which were captured by the British Navy, and provides a list of commanding officers who were killed during this period. This volume presents a valuable summary of the major actions and prizes the British Navy fought and captured during this early period of the Revolutionary Wars.

Cambridge University Press has long been a pioneer in the reissuing of out-of-print titles from its own backlist, producing digital reprints of books that are still sought after by scholars and students but could not be reprinted economically using traditional technology. The Cambridge Library Collection extends this activity to a wider range of books which are still of importance to researchers and professionals, either for the source material they contain, or as landmarks in the history of their academic discipline.

Drawing from the world-renowned collections in the Cambridge University Library, and guided by the advice of experts in each subject area, Cambridge University Press is using state-of-the-art scanning machines in its own Printing House to capture the content of each book selected for inclusion. The files are processed to give a consistently clear, crisp image, and the books finished to the high quality standard for which the Press is recognised around the world. The latest print-on-demand technology ensures that the books will remain available indefinitely, and that orders for single or multiple copies can quickly be supplied.

The Cambridge Library Collection will bring back to life books of enduring scholarly value (including out-of-copyright works originally issued by other publishers) across a wide range of disciplines in the humanities and social sciences and in science and technology.

Steel's Naval Remembrancer

*From the Commencement of the War
in 1793 to the End of the Year 1800*

DAVID STEEL

CAMBRIDGE
UNIVERSITY PRESS

CAMBRIDGE UNIVERSITY PRESS

Cambridge, New York, Melbourne, Madrid, Cape Town, Singapore,
São Paolo, Delhi, Dubai, Tokyo, Mexico City

Published in the United States of America by Cambridge University Press, New York

www.cambridge.org
Information on this title: www.cambridge.org/9781108023771

© in this compilation Cambridge University Press 2010

This edition first published 1801
This digitally printed version 2010

ISBN 978-1-108-02377-1 Paperback

STEEL's
NAVAL REMEMBRANCER,

FROM THE

COMMENCEMENT of the WAR,

IN 1793,

To the End of the Year 1800.

A Reprefentation of the MEDAL prefented by the KING to thofe Flag-Officers and Captains of Ships of the Line who particularly fignalized themfelves in the Four Grand Engagements under the following Commanders-in-Chief.

Admiral

EARL HOWE,

1ft June,

1794.

Admiral

A. DUNCAN,

11th October,

1797.

Admiral

Sir J. JERVIS,
K. B.

14th February,

1797.

Rear-Admiral

Sir H. NELSON,
K. B.

1ft August,

1798.

On the obverfe Side of th
of Oak and Laurel, a
Officer and the Date

Medal, within the Wreath
infcribed the Name of the
the Engagement.

STEEL's
NAVAL REMEMBRANCER,

FROM THE COMMENCEMENT OF THE WAR IN 1793
TO THE END OF THE YEAR 1800:

Intended as a complete Supplement to the Navy-Lifts up to that Period:

AND CONTAINING

An Account of all the Ships of the FRENCH, DUTCH, SPANISH, and BRITISH, Navies, loft, taken, or deftroyed, fince the Commencement of the prefent War, to December 31, 1800; accompanied with brief but moft accurate Narratives of the Circumftances attendant on each Event.

A complete Lift, for the fame Period, of all the FRENCH, DUTCH, and SPANISH, PRIVATEERS, taken by Great Britain, with the Force of each, the Names of the Captors, &c.

A chronological Lift of thofe SETTLEMENTS and COLONIES captured from the Enemy in which the Navy have had a Share; with the Names of the Ships concerned in the refpective Captures.

A GENERAL STATEMENT or Recapitulation of Captures in Ships and Guns. And

A Lift of the BRITISH COMMANDING-OFFICERS, who have loft their Lives in the Service of their Country, beginning with the prefent War, and ending on December 31, 1800.

LONDON:

PRINTED FOR DAVID STEEL, AT HIS NAVIGATION-WAREHOUSE, No. 1, UNION-ROW, MINORIES, LITTLE TOWER-HILL:

And fold by the following Bookfellers, viz. Mr. FOURDRINIER, 20, Charing-Crofs; Mr. St. JOHN, Strand; Mr. REED, 444, Strand; Mr. TINDAL, 112, Great Portland-Street; Meffrs. HODGSONS, Wimpole-Street; Mr DEBRETT, Picadilly; Mr. CHAPPLE, Pall Mall; Mr. WESTLEY, 159, Strand; Mr. JORDAN, Fleet-Street; the Bookfellers in Pater-Noiter-Row; Mr. HESKETT, Royal-Exchange; Mr. DONALDSON, Mr. WHITEWOOD, Mr. MATTHEWS, Mr. MILLS, Mr. WOODWARD, Mr. GUEST, and Mr. MOTTLEY, Portfmouth; Mr. TARRING, Brixham-Quay, Torbay; Mr. CONGDON and Mr. HOXLAND, Plymouth-Dock; Mr. RICHARDS, and Mr. BARNIKEL, Plymouth; Mr. MOORE, Poole; Mrs. DOHERTY, Falmouth; Mr. JACKSON, Dartmouth; Mr. WOOD, Weymouth; Mr. POTTER, Printer, Haverfordweft; Mrs. THORN, Dorchefter; Mr. W. HARDING, and Mr. WATTS, Gofport; Mr. W. BROWNE on tne Tolzey, Briftol; Mr. JOHN REED Wine-Street, Briftol; Mr. SEAGER, Harwich; Mr. DOWNES, Yarmouth; Mr. J. HEDLEY, Lynn; Mr. EDWARDS, Woolwich: Mr. T WNSON, and Mr. ETHERINGTON, Chatham; Mr. GASKIN and BRYAN, Sheernefs; Mr. DONALDSON and WILKES, Brighton; Mr. ETHERINGTON, Rochefter; Mr. CURLING, and Mr. HAWKES, Deptford; and the other Bookfellers in Town and Country.

Printed by H. L. Galabin, Ingram-Court, Fenchurch-Street, London.

CONTRACTIONS and CHARACTERS EXPLAINED.

* This character denotes that the ship's name to which it is affixed was in the British service at the close of the year 1800.

F. French.   *D.* Dutch.   *S.* Spanish.
B. Built.   *T.* Taken.   *P.* Purchased.

———————

THE FOLLOWING CAPTURES HAVE BEEN ANNOUNCED SINCE THIS WORK WAS PUT TO PRESS.

LA CONCORDE, *F.* 44: Taken by the Belliqueux, 64, R. Bulteel, near Rio Janeiro, South America, August 5, 1800.

LA MEDEE, 36 : Taken by the Bombay-Castle, Indiaman, J. Hamilton ; and Exeter, ditto, H. Meriton ; part of the convoy under the Belliqueux, 64, above-mentioned, in the evening of the same day.

Several other frigates are said to have been lately taken in the East Indies, but they have not yet been officially announced.

———————

E R R A T A, &c.

PAGE.

1 La Cleopatra, annex the date, *June* 19.

6 For " Vallaret Joyeuse" read " Villaret de Joyeuse."

8 La Pique, 38, insert in the West Indies.

12 For " L'Amanranthe" read " L'Amaranthe."

22 Annex a * to La Cruelle.

23 For " a Sloop, name unknown," read " Le Quiproquo."

[Entered at Stationers' Hall.]

PREFACE.

THE triumphs of the British Navy, from the time of Alfred down to the close of the eighteenth century, were never greater than those in the present war. In fleets or in single combats, victory or fame have had something to record. Skill, perseverance, courage, high honour, and generous feeling, have been the characteristics of the naval warriors of Britain in the present contest. And, although History will fix upon the greater and more brilliant epochs, although she will consecrate to latest time the fame of Howe, of Jervis, of Duncan, and of Nelson, and shade their brows with the laurel of victory; not less deserving of record are acts of individual heroism and gallantry, such as were exhibited by Faulknor in the West Indies, and by Hood on the shores of hostile France. The remembrance of these deeds affects the sympathy of a nation, and acts as a stimulus to a new race of heroes. Emulation (oh! how unlike ambition!) inflames the latent spark of honourable sensation, governs the noble mind, and leads it on by means of high example : — " Such are the sons of Britain."

This work records our naval occurrences from the commencement of the present war to the close of the year 1800. More circumstances than one led to the adoption of this period. A new and nearer political connexion then took place between Great Britain and Ireland; and a great confederacy had then just been entered into between the northern powers, which threatened this country with an increase of her enemies. Thus, the internal and external relations of Great Britain were changed; and, from this dividing point of time and circumstance, it was thought not improper nor inconvenient to take a retrospection. It is compiled with the most scrupulous attention to accuracy, and from sources peculiar to the publisher, who has long devoted his attention to the concerns of the British Navy. It forms a complete supplement to the Navy-Lists to that period : and henceforward the captures, both of national ships and privateers, will be continued every month in Steel's List of the Royal Navy.

COMMANDING-OFFICERS

Who have loſt their Lives in the Service of Great Britain during the preſent War.

b ſignifies blown up, — d drowned, — k killed.

NAMES.	Rk	made	Ships they command.		died
GEO. W. Aug. Courtney k	PC	1782	Bofton - - - -	32	1793
Ab. Pulliblank - d	L	1782	Pigmy (Cut.) - -	14	1793
H.T.H.Maitland k	L	1793	Spitfire - - - -	14	1793
James Cook - - d	C	1793	Spitfire (Sp) - -	1	1794
T. W. Rich - - d	C		Spitfire (Sch.) -	8	1794
James Miln - - k	L	1793	Avenger (Sp) - -	16	1794
James Montagu k	PC	1775	Montague - - -	74	1794
John Harvey - - k	PC	1777	Brunfwick - - -	74	1794
R. M. Sutton - - d	PC	1779	Ardent - - - -	64	1794
John Hutt - - - k	PC	1783	Oueen - - - -	98	1794
Lewis Robertfon k	PC	1782	Veteran - - -	64	1794
Walter Serocold k	C		At a battery agft Calvi		1794
R. Faulknor - - k	PC	1794	Blanche - - - -	32	1795
Adam Littlejohn k	PC	1795	Berwick - - - -	74	1795
James M Carthy d	L	1795	Mufquito (GV) -	5	1795
Hon. R. Forbes d	PC	1790	Dryad - - - -	36	1795
John Woodley - d	PC	1793	Leda - - - - -	36	1795
S. Seymour - - d	C	1795	Arab - - - - -	18	1796
W. Swaffield - - b	PC	1793	in Amphion,onaVifit	32	1796
C. Garnier - - - d	C	1795	Aurora - - - -	28	1796
J. J. Symon - - - d	C		Helena (Sp) - -	18	1796
T. Gott - - - - d	L		Cormorant(blwnup)	16	1796
T. Maxtone - - - d	C	1790	Bermuda - - - -	18	1796
F. V. Field - - - d	C	1795	Curlew (Bg) - - -	18	1796
J. Guerin - - - - d	C	1794	La Sirenne - - -	16	1796
William Mulfo - d	C	1796	Hermes - - - -	14	1797
John Smith - - - d	C	1795	Ld Mulgrave (ASS)	20	1797
J. H. Parker - - d	C	1796	La Vipere - - -	18	1797
Richard Bowen - k	PC	1794	Terpfichore - - -	32	1797
J. Giblon - - - - k	L		Fox, (Cut.) - - -	12	1797
Wm Huggett - - d	L	179c	Refolution (Bg) -	14	1797
Wm Gordall - - d	L		Grace (RB) - - -	3	1797
R.R.und Burgefs k	PC	1790	Ardent - - - - -	64	1797
H.Pigot k byCrew	PC	1794	Hermione - - - -	32	1797
R. Parker - - - d	PC	1790	Intrepid - - - -	64	1797
John M'Inethenyk	L	1795	Marie Antoinette -	1	1797
J. Hollingfworth k	L	1793	Growler (GV) - -	12	1797
Scory Barker - - d	PC	1793	Wr. in Le Tribune	44	1797
Samuel Mafon - d	L	1783	Pandour (Bg) - -	14	1797
ThomasHayward d	C	1796	Swift (Sp) - - -	16	1797
John Drew - - - d	PC	1797	Cerberus - - - -	32	1798
J. K. Pulling - - d	PC	1797	Form. of the Penguin	18	1798
Horace Pine - - d	C	1794	Scorpion (Sp) - -	16	1798
Alexander Hood k	PC	1781	Mars - - - - -	74	1798
Roger Mears - - d	C	1794	Mackarel Tran/port		
James Drew - - d	C	1790	De Braak (Cut.) -	14	1798
G. B. Weftcott - k	PC	1790	Majeftic - - - -	74	1798
John Pollexfen - d	L	1795	Margaret (Tender)	—	1798
Whittle - - d	L		Caroline (Tender)	—	1798
Lewis Mortlock k	C	1798	Woolverene (GV)	12	1799
Hon. H Grey - d	C	1798	Weazle (Sp) - -	12	1799
Sir C. Linday, Btd	PC	1797	Daphne - - - -	20	1799
D. Willmott - - k	PC	1798	Alliance (Sp) - -	20	1799
E. Pakenham - b	PC	179c	Refiftance - - -	44	1799
R. W. Miller - - b	PC	1796	Thefeus - - - -	74	1799
L. Skynner - - - d	PC	1795	La Lutine - - -	32	1799
Edw. Cooke- - k	PC	1794	La Sybile - - -	44	1799
Valent. Edwards d	PC	1787	Sceptre - - - -	64	1799
John Rowe - - b	C	1790	Trincomalé (Sp) -	16	1799
James Hanfon - d	C	1795	Brazen (Sp) - - -	18	1800
Andrew Todd - b	PC	1796	Queen Charlotte	100	1800
J. P. Robinfon - d	C	1796	Trompeufe - - -	18	1800
John Raynor - d	C	1796	Railleur - - - -	20	1800
W. J. Turquand d	C	1798	Hound (Bg) - -	18	1800
G. S. Stovin - - d	C	1800	Chance (lateGalgo)	16	1800

FRENCH NATIONAL SHIPS

LOST, TAKEN, or DESTROYED.

WAR was decreed by France, againſt Britain, February 1, 1793; *and His Majeſty's Proclamation, for making Repriſals, was dated on the* 11*th of the ſame Month.*

1793.

LE LEOPARD, 74: Loſt in the Bay of Cagliari, Sardinia, February 15.

LE GŒLAN, 14: Taken by the Penelope, 36, B. S. Rowley, Jamaica-ſtation, April 16.

*LA PROMPTE, 20: Taken by the Phaëton, 38, Sir A. S. Douglas, off the coaſt of Spain, May 28.

LE CURIEUX, (brig,) 14: Taken by the Inconſtant, 36, A. Montgomery, Weſt Indies, June 3.

LE VANNEAU, 6: Taken by the Coloſſus, 74, C. M. Pole, in the Bay of Bifcay, June 6. Afterwards in the Britiſh ſervice, and loſt November, 1796. — *See Britiſh ſhips loſt, &c.*

*LA CLEOPATRE, (now L Oiſeau, 36,) 40: Taken by La Nymphe, 36, E. Pellew, off the Start, after a ſevere action of 55 minutes, in which the Britiſh boarded and ſtruck the flag of La Cléopatre. The loſs of the enemy was about 60 in killed and wounded, beſides the captain, Jean Mullon, killed. That of the Britiſh, 23 killed and 27 wounded. For his admirable conduct in this action, Captain Pellew received the honour of knighthood.

*L'ECLAIR, 22: Taken by the Leda, 32, G. Campbell, Mediterranean, June 9.

LUTINE, (ſloop,) 12: Taken by the Pluto, 14, J. N. Morris, Newfoundland, July 25.

LA CONVENTION NATIONALE, (ſchooner,) 10: Taken by Commodore Ford's ſquadron, St. Domingo, in September. Afterwards named *Marie Antoinette* in the Britiſh ſervice, and run away with by the crew in the Weſt Indies, 1797. — *See Britiſh ſhips loſt, &c.*

*LA MODESTE, (now 38,) 36 : Taken by the Bedford, 74, R. Man and others, out of Genoa, in the Mediterranean, October 17.

LA REUNION, 36 : Taken by the Crescent, 36, J. Saumarez, off Cherbourg, October 20, after a close action of two hours and ten minutes without the lofs of a man killed or one wounded. (The Circe, 28, J. S. Yorke, in fight.) The enemy had 120 killed and wounded. The ship was afterwards taken into the British fervice, and loft December 7, 1796. *See British ships loft, &c.* Captain Saumarez for his gallant conduct in this action received the honour of knighthood.

L'INCONSTANTE, 36 : Taken by the Penelope, 36, B. S. Rowley, and Iphigenia, 32, P. Sinclair, in the Bight of Leogane, St. Domingo, Nov. 25. Afterwards taken into the British fervice, named the *Convert*, and loft March 8, 1794. *.See British ships loft, &c.*

LE SCIPION, 74 : Took fire and blew up in Leghorn-Roads, November 26.

LA BLONDE, (corvette,) 28 : Taken by the Latona, 32, E. Thornborough, and Phaeton 38, Sir A. S. Douglas, off Ufhant, November 27.

*L'ESPIEGLE, (floop,) 16 : Taken by La Nymphe, 36, I. Pellew, *(acting,)* and Circe, 28, J. S. Yorke, near Ufhant, November 30.

LE TRIOMPHANT,	84 :	Burnt in the grand arfenal at Toulon, December 18, 1793, by the Vulcan, F. S. 14, Capt. C. Hare, under orders from Sir W. S. Smith, knt. who was appointed to conduct the deftroying of the French ships there by Admiral Lord Hood.
DU GUAY TROUIN,	74 :	
LE DESTIN,	74 :	
LE LYS,	74 :	
LA SUFFISANTE,	76 :	
LA SERIEUSE,	36 :	
L'IPHIGENIE,	34 :	
L'AUGUSTE,	24 :	

LE COMMERCE DE BOUR-DEAUX, 84 : Burnt, under fimilar orders, by Lieut. Middleton of the Britannia, and Lieut. Jones Stiles of the Windfor-
LE CENTAUR, 74 : Caftle.

LE DICTATEUR, 74 : Burnt, under fimilar orders, by Lieut. R. W. Miller of the Wind-for-Caftle.

LE THEMISTOCLE, 74 : Burnt, under fimilar orders, in the inner road, by Lieut. Pa-
LE HEROS, 74 : ter of the Britannia, and Lieut. R. W. Miller.

A SHIP BUILDING, 74. Burnt, under fimilar orders, in the dock-yard, by Capt.
A FRIGATE BUILDING, 36 : W. Edge of the Alert, (floop,) and Lieut. C. Tup-
LA CAROLINE, 24 : per of the Victory.
L'ALERTE, 18 :

LE MONTREAL, *(powder-maga-zine,)* 32 : Burnt, by miftake, by the Spaniards, in the inner road, inftead of being funk, and blew up with a
L'IRIS, *(powder-magazine,)* 32 : dreadful explofion.

LA VICTOIRE, 32 : Burnt, by the Sardinians, on fhore, in getting out of the arfenal.

*** La Sérieufe, 36 ; L'Alerte, 18 ; L'Iphigénie, 34 ; Le Commerce de Bourdeaux, 84 ; the 74-gun ship and the frigate of 36 building ; were not deftroyed fo as to prevent repair.

*LE

*LE COMMERCE DE MARSEILLES, 120 : ⎫ Brought away from Toulon, December
*LE PUISSANT,   74 :   ⎪ 18, under the command of Admiral
*LE POMPEE,   80 :   ⎪ Lord Hood ; there being then left in
L'ARETHUSE,   40 :   ⎪ that port, undeftroyed, one of 120,
LA PERLE,   36 :   ⎪ three of 80, eight of 74, two of 32,
*LA TOPAZE,   38 :   ⎪ and one of 24. Of thefe fhips, after-
*L'AURORE,   32 :   ⎬ wards in the Britifh fervice, L'Aré-
LA LUTINE,   32 :   ⎪ thufe *(afterwards Undaunted)* founder-
LA POULETTE,   26 :   ⎪ ed in the Weft Indies, Auguft 27,
LA BELETTE,   24 :   ⎪ 1796 ; La Perle *(afterwards Amethyft)*
LA PROSELYTE,   24 :   ⎪ was loft at Alderney, December 29,
LA MOZELLE,   20 :   ⎪ 1795 ; La Lutine was loft on the coaft
LA MULETTE,   18 :   ⎪ of Holland, Oftober 9, 1799 ; La
LA SINCERE,   18 :   ⎪ Poulette and La Belette were burnt
LE TARLESTON,   14 :   ⎭ at Ajaccio, being unferviceable, Ofto-
ber 20, 1796 ; La Profélyte was funk, at the fiege of Baftia, in May, 1794 ; La Mozelle
was retaken at Toulon, January 7, 1794, and again taken as hereafter-mentioned. *See Bri-
tifh fhips loft, &c.* Admiral Lord Hood, his officers, and feamen, for their meritorious con-
duft at Toulon, &c. received the thanks of both Houfes of Parliament.

L'ALCESTE, 32 : Surrendered at Toulon, and retained by the Sardinians, Dec.

L'EMBROYE, 20 : Surrendered at Toulon, and retained by the Neapolitans, Dec.

LE PETIT AURORE, 18 : Surrendered at Toulon, and retained by the Spaniards, Dec.

*L'IMPERIEUSE, 40 : Taken by a fquadron, under Vice-Admiral John Gell, out of
E'Specia, in the ftate of Genoa, October 11.

LE VENGEUR, (floop,)   12 : ⎫ Taken by the Blanche, 32, C. Parker, in the Weft In-
LA REVOLUTIONAIRE, 20 : ⎬ dies, Dec. 30.
LE SANS CULOTTES,   22 : ⎭

1794.

LA TROMPEUSE, (brig,) 18 : Taken by the Sphynx, 20, R. Lucas, off Cape Clear,
January 12. Afterwards in the Britifh fervice, and loft near Kinfale, June, 1796. *See Britifh fhips loft, &c.*

LA VIPERE, (brig,) 16 : Taken by the Flora, 36, Sir J. B. Warren, in the Channel,
January 23. Afterwards in the Britifh fervice, and loft off the Shannon, January 2, 1797. *See
Britifh fhips loft, &c.*

*LA MINERVE, *(now St. Fiorenzo,)* 40 : Sunk at St. Fiorenzo, Corfica, by the Englifh
batteries, Feb. 19 ; but afterwards weighed and commiffioned.

FORTUNEE, 44 : Sunk at St. Fiorenzo, Corfica, by the Englifh batteries, Feb. 19.

L'ACTIF and *L'ESPIEGLE, 12 : Taken by the Iphigenia, 32, P. Sinclair, Weft Indies, March 16. L'Aftif was afterwards in the Britifh fervice, and foundered off Bermuda,
Nov. 26, 1794. *See Britifh fhips loft, &c.*

BIEN

BIEN VENU, 32: Taken by Vice-Admiral Sir John Jervis's squadron, at Martinico, March 17. Afterwards named *Undaunted* in the British service, *and lost.*

*AVENGER, (sloop,) 16: Taken by Vice-Admiral Sir J. Jervis's squadron at Martinico, March 17.

LA LIBERTE', 14: Taken by the Alligator, 28, T Surridge, near Jamaica, March 28.

*LA POMONE, 44: } Taken by the Flora, 36, Sir J. B. Warren, Melampus, 36, T Wells,
*LE BABET,   20: } and Aréthufe, 38, Sir E. Pellew, off the Isle of Bas, Channel, April 23, after an action of nearly three hours. The French squadron confisted of L'Engageant, 38; La Pomone, 44; Réfolué, 36; and Babet, 22. La Réfolue made her efcape by fwift failing. The Britifh had 11 killed and 13 wounded in the three fhips. The enemy nearly 130 killed and wounded in the Pomone and Babet. The Pomone was fuppofed to be the fineft frigate in the French fervice. The Concorde came up at the clofe of the action, and, joining in purfuit, captured as follows:

*L'ENGAGEANTE, 38: Taken by the Concorde, 36, Sir R. J. Strachan, bart. after an engagement of two hours and a half, in the Channel, April 23. The Nymphe and Melampus, returning from the chafe of the Réfolue above-mentioned, fell in with the Concorde after the engagement, and affifted the difabled fhips.

GUADALOUPE, (sloop,) 16: Taken by the squadron under Vice-Admiral Sir J. Jervis, K. B. at Guadaloupe, April 23.

LA DU GUAY TROUIN, 34: Formerly the Princefs Royal, Englifh Eaft-India fhip. Taken by the Orpheus, 32, H. Newcome, Eaft Indies, May 5, after a fharp engagement of one hour and ten minutes. The Britifh had one killed and nine wounded. The enemy 21 killed and 60 wounded. The Centurion, 50, S. Ofborne, and Refiftance, 44, E. Pakenham, came in fight when the fhip ftruck.

L ATALANTE, 38: Taken by the Swiftfure, 74, C. Boyles, Irifh ftation, May. Afterwards in the Britifh fervice, named L'Efpion, and loft on the Goodwin-Sands, November 16, 1799. *See British ships lost, &c.*

LA FLECHE, 14: Taken by the fleet under Admiral Lord Hood, at Baftia, Corfica, May 21. Afterwards in the Britifh fervice, and loft in St. Fiorenzo-Bay, November 12, 1795. *See British ships lost, &c.*

LA COURIER, (cutter,) 10: Taken and fcuttled by the fleet under Admiral Earl Howe, in the Channel, May 23.

LA REPUBLIQUAIN, 20: } Taken and burnt by the fleet under Admiral Earl Howe, in
L'INCONNUE, (brig,) 16: } the Channel, May 25.

*CASTOR, 32: Captured from the Britifh, May 9, 1794. *See British ships lost, &c.* Retaken by the Carysfort, 28, F. Laforey, after an action of one hour and 15 minutes, off the Land's End, May 29. The Carysfort had one killed and fix wounded; the Caftor 16 killed and nine wounded.

LA MOSELLE, 20: Taken by L'Aimable, 32, Sir H. Burrard, off the Hieres Iflands in the Mediterranean. May 23.

*LE

*LE JUSTE,   80: ⎫ Taken by the fleet under the Right Hon. Richard Earl
*SANS PAREIL,   80: ⎪ Howe, Vice-Admiral of England, Ufhant bearing E.
*L'AMERICA, (now *L'Im-* ⎰ half N. about 150 leagues diftant, June 1. The fol-
pétueux,)   78: ⎱ lowing are the names of the fhips which compofed the
L'ACHILLE,   74: ⎰ line of battle on that memorable day, with the names
NORTHUMBERLAND, 74: ⎱ of their commanders, and the numbers of killed and
L'IMPETUEUX,   78: ⎱ wounded in each, including officers, viz. Alfred, 74,
LE VENGEUR,   74: ⎰ J. Bazely, 0 k. 8 w. — Barfleur, 98, *Rear-Admiral
G. Bowyer, Capt. C. Collingwood, 9 k. 29 w. — Bellerophon, 74, *Rear-Admiral T. Paf-
ley, *Capt. W. Hope, 4 k. 30 w. — Brunfwick, 74, J. Harvey, 33 k. 93 w. — Cæfar, 80,
A. J. Molloy, 18 k. 37 w. — Culloden, 74, If. Schomberg, 2 k. 5 w. — Defence, 74, *J.
Gambier, 20 k. 41 w. — Gibraltar, 80, T. Mackenzie, 2 k. 12 w. — Glory, 98, *J. El-
phinftone, 15 k. 39 w. — Impregnable, 98, Rear-Admiral B. Caldwell, Capt. G. B. Weft-
cott, 8 k. 26 w. — Invincible, 74, *Hon. T. Pakenham, 14 k. 31 w. — Leviathan, 74,
*Lord Hugh Seymour, 10 k. 34 w. — Majeftic, 74, Charles Cotton, 3 k. 5 w. — Marlbo-
rough, 74, Hon. G. Berkley, 30 k. 98 w. — Montague, 74, J. Montagu, 5 k. 15 w. —
Orion, 74, *J. T. Duckworth, 5 k. 24 w. — Queen, 98, *Rear-Admiral A. Gardner, Capt. J.
Hutt, 38 k. 74 w. — Queen Charlotte, 100, *Admiral Earl Howe, *Rear-Admiral Sir R.
Curtis, and *Capt. Sir A. S. Douglas, 16 k. 14 w. — Ramillies, 74, *H. Harvey, 2 k. 7 w.
— Royal George, 100, *Vice-Admiral Sir Alexander Hood, *Capt. W. Domett, 22 k. 76 w.
— Royal Sovereign, 100, *Vice-Admiral T. Graves, *Capt. H. Nicholls, 15 k. 47 w. —
Ruffel, 74, *J. W. Payne, 8 k. 29 w. — Thunderer, 74, A. Bertie, none k. or w. — Tre-
mendous, 74, J. Pigott, 4 k. 8 w. — And Valiant, 74, *T. Pringle, 2 k. 9 w. — Of the officers
and foldiers of the 29th regiment, who were on-board the fleet, 12 k. and 20 w. — The total
number of Britifh killed and wounded in the 25 fhips was, therefore, 297 k. and 811 w.
The French line confifted of 26 fhips ; of their lofs we poffefs no accurate account, but it muft
have been immenfe. — The following are the numbers of killed and wounded in the fhips taken : Le Jufte, 100 k. 145 w. — Sans Pareil, 260 k. 120 w. — L'America, 134 k. 110 w.
— L'Achille, 36 k. 30 w. — Northumberland, 60 k. 100 w. — L'Impétueux, 100 k. 75 w.
— Le Vengeur funk, foon after fhe had ftruck, with 625 fouls. — Total 690 k. 625 drowned,
and 580 w. in the fhips captured.
    The following frigates, &c. attended the Britifh fleet, viz. Phaeton, 38, W. Bentinck ;
Niger, 32, *repeater*, Hon. A. K. Legge ; Latona, 38, E. Thornbrough ; Southampton, 32,
Hon. R. Forbes ; Venus, 32, W. Brown ; Aquilon, 32, *repeater*, Hon. R. Stopford ; Pegafus,
28, *repeater*, R. Barlow ; Charon, (H. S.) 44, G. Countefs ; Comet, (F. S.) 14, W. Bradley ;
Incendiary, (F. S.) 14, J. Cooke, (1,) ; King's Fifher, (floop,) 18, T. Le M. Goffelin ;
Ranger, (cutter,) 14, Lieut. C. Cotgrave ; and Rattler, (cutter,) 14, Lieut. J. Wynne.
    The French fleet was firft defcried in the morning of the 28th of May, by the advanced fri-
gates, far diftant on the weather-bow ; and, about 8 o'clock, they were feen by the fleet in
latitude 47 deg. 33 min. N. longitude 14 deg. 10 min. W. when the wind was frefh from
the S. W. and the fea very rough. A general chafe to the eaftward commenced, which con-

tinued until the evening. At the clofe of the day, Rear-Admiral Pafley led on his divifion, and attacked the Révolutionnaire, of 110 guns, the fternmoft fhip of the enemy s line ; but foon after, having a topmaft difabled, the Leviathan pufhed up along-fide and engaged that fhip. *She* was relieved by the Audacious, 74, *W. Parker, and ftretched on a-head. The Audacious continued the action for two hours, and totally difmafted the enemy's fhip, which ftruck. A dark night then enfued, and the Révolutionnaire efcaped. In the morning, the Audacious, then in a fhattered ftate, was attacked by a large frigate and two corvettes, and obliged to return to port to refit. The Audacious had 4 killed and 18 wounded.

The two fleets, in the night of the 28th, continued on the ftarboard-tack in a parallel direction, the French ftill to windward ; and the next day a partial action took place, in which the French line was broken by the Queen Charlotte and Bellerophon. The enemy then wore, and the Britifh gained the wind. The Royal George and Queen, with feveral of the rear fhips, were, on this day, much difabled. On the next two days, the 30th and 31ft, a thick fog prevailed, and the enemy were feen, at intervals, a few miles diftant ; but, clearing up in the afternoon of the 31ft, at 7 in the evening of that day, the Britifh having the weather-gage, both fleets were in order of battle, and, in lefs than an hour after day-light next morning, (June 1,) clofe action commenced in the centre. How the battle was contefted on that day, it is needlefs to defcribe. In the afternoon, the French Admiral, Vallaret Joyeufe, who had been engaged by the Queen Charlotte, crowded off, and was followed by moft of the fhips of his van in condition to carry fail, leaving with the Britifh 10 or 12 of his crippled and difmafted fhips ; but the greater number of the Britifh fhips were at this time fo difabled or feparated as to be incapable of preventing the efcape of two or three of them, and thofe only remained which we have enumerated.

Capt. J. Montagu was killed ; Captains J. Harvey and J. Hutt died fhortly after of their wounds. Admiral Graves was wounded in the arm ; and Rear-Admirals Bowyer and Pafley loft a leg ; in confideration of which, a penfion of £1000 per ann. was given to each of thefe officers for their meritorious fervices. The two houfes of parliament voted their thanks to Earl Howe, his officers, and feamen. Earl Howe was alfo prefented with a diamond-hilted fword of great value, by the King in perfon, on-board at Spithead, and with a golden chain to which a medal was appended commemorative of this event. Admirals Graves and Sir Alexander Hood had each the honour of a peerage ; and Rear-Admirals Bowyer and Pafley were created b·ronets ; befides which, in December, 1796, there was prefented, by order of his Majefty, to each of the flag-officers and fuch of the captains as were reported by Earl Howe to have *particularly* fignalized themfelves in the engagement, a gold medal and chain to the flag-officers, and a gold medal to the captains, to be worn when they wear their uniforms. The flag-officer's fufpended by a blue-and-white ribbon round the neck, and the captain's in the third and fourth button-hole on their left fide. The names of the officers to whom medals were prefented are diftinguifhed above by this mark *. —— L'Impétueux was burnt by accident in Portfmouth-Harbour, Auguft 29, 1794. *See Britifh fhip loft, &c.*

*LA SYBILLE, 44 : Taken by the Romney, 50. Hon. W. Paget, at Miconi, Mediterranean, after an action of one hour and ten minutes, June 17.

NARCISSE, (cutter,) 14 : Taken by the Aurora, 28, W. Effington, off Shetland, June 18.

*LA MELPOMENE, 44 : ⎫ Taken by the fleet under Lord Hood in the Harbour of
LA MIGNONNE, 32 : ⎪ Calvi, Corfica, Auguft 10. La Mignonne, afterwards
L'AUGUSTE, (brig,) 4 : ⎬ in the Britifh fervice, was burnt, as unferviceable, at
PROVIDENCE, (brig,) 4 : ⎪ Ferrajo, July 31, 1797.
CA IRA, (gun-boat,) 3 : ⎭

VOLUNTAIRE, 40 : Run on-fhore and deftroyed near the rocks called the Penmarks, coaft of France, by part of Sir. J. B. Warren's fquadron, Auguft 23. *This ſhip, in the Gazette account, was called La Félicité.*

ALERT, 18 : Run on-fhore and deftroyed near Point-du-Raz, 9 leagues from Breft, by part of Sir J. B. Warren's fquadron, Auguft 23. This fhip was formerly Britifh. *See Britiſh ſhips loſt, &c. — Commodore Sir J. B. Warren alſo run a-ground, at the ſame time, L'Eſpion, 18, which appears to have been refitted, and ſubſequently captured, as ſtated hereafter.*

LA SIRENNE, (floop,) 16 : Taken by the Intrepid, 64, Hon. C. Carpenter, and Chi-chefter, 44, R. D. Fancourt, on the coaft of St. Domingo, in Auguft. Afterwards in the Britifh fervice, and loft in Auguft, 1796. — *See Britiſh ſhips loſt, &c.*

REPRISAL, 16 : Taken by the fquadron under Sir J. Jervis, K. B. in the Weft Indies.

QUARTIDI, 14 : Taken by Sir Edward Pellew's fquadron, off Scilly, September 7.

*LE JACOBIN, (*now Matilda*,) 24 : Taken by the Ganges, 74, W. Trufcott, and Montague, 74, W. Fooks, in the Weft Indies, Octoher 30.

*LA REVOLUTIONNAIRE, 44 : Taken by the Artois, 38, E. Nagle, in company with the Arethufa, 38, Sir E. Pellew ; Diamond, 38, Sir W. S. Smith ; and Galatea, 32, R. G. Keats ; about 10 leagues from Breft, October 21.

*REVENGE, (corvette,) (*now Hobart*,) 18 : Taken by the Refiftance, 44, E. Pakenham, in the Straits of Sunda.

LA CARMAGNOLE, (fchooner,) 10 : Taken by the Zebra, 16, off St. Lucia, Weft Indies, Nov. 30

A SLOOP, (*name unknown*) : Taken by the Beaulieu, 40, E. Riou, Weft Indies, Dec. 2.

LE REVOLUTIONNAIRE, 110 : Loft on the Mingan-Rock, in returning to Breft, December 27.

A LARGE SCHOONER, (*name unknown*) : Chafed into the Bay of Defeada, Weft Indies, and captured there under a battery, by the Blanche, 32, R. Faulknor, Dec. 30.

1795.

LE NEPTUNE, 80: Caft away in the bay of Hodierne, coaft of France, January.

LE SCIPION, 80 : ⎫
LE NEUF THERMIDOR, 80 : ⎬ Foundered in a gale of wind, January.
LA SUPERBE, 74 : ⎭

LE DURAS, 20 : Taken by the Bellona, 74, G. Wilfon, and Alarm, 32, J. Carpenter, Weft Indies, January.

LA DUQUESNE, 44 : Taken by the Bellona, 74, G. Wilfon, in the Weft Indies, January 5.   LA

LA PIQUE, 38 : Taken by the Blanche, 32, R. Faulknor, after a moſt brilliant engagement of five hours, which exhibited an equal diſplay of ſkill and courage. The gallant Captain Faulknor fell two hours after the action began, which was then continued with the moſt determined bravery by Lieut. F. Watkins. The loſs of the French was not leſs than 200 in killed and wounded ; that of the Britiſh 8 killed and 21 wounded. La Pique was afterwards in the Britiſh ſervice, and loſt June 29, 1798. — *See Britiſh ſhips loſt, &c.*

L'ESPERANCE, 22 : Taken by the Argonaut, 64, A. J. Ball, on the coaſt of America, Jan. 8.

L'IPHIGENIE, 32 : Taken by the Spaniſh ſquadron, under Admiral Langara, Mediterranean, February 10.

LA CURIEUSE, (ſchooner,) 12 : Taken by the Pomone, 44, Sir J. B. Warren, off the Iſle of Grouis, coaſt of France, February 26.

*REQUIN, (A. B.) 12 : Taken by the Thalia, 36, R. Grindall, Channel ſtation, Feb.

*L'ESPION, (*now Spy*,) 18 : Taken by the Lively, 32, G. Burlton, off Breſt, March 2.

*LA TOURTERELLE, 30 : Taken by the Lively, 32, G. Burlton, 13 leagues from Uſhant, March 13.

CENSEUR, 74, and CA IRA, 80 : Taken, from to leeward of the French fleet, to which they belonged, conſiſting of fifteen ſhips of the line, five frigates, and one ſloop, by the fleet under Vice-Admiral W. Hotham, conſiſting of fourteen of the line, eight frigates, and a cutter, off Genoa, March 14. The Cenſeur had, when captured, 1000 men on-board ; the Ca Ira 1300. They loſt, in killed and wounded, between 300 and 400. Theſe ſhips were afterwards in the Britiſh ſervice : the former was retaken by the French fleet, Oct. 7, 1795, and the latter was burnt by accident, April 11, 1796. — *See Britiſh ſhips loſt, &c.*

TEMERAIRE, (cutter,) 20 : Taken by the Dido, 28, G. H. Towry, Mediterranean.

REPUBLIQUAINE, (corvette,) 22 : Taken by the ſquadron under Rear-Admiral J. Colpoys, Channel ſtation, March 27.

SPEEDY, (ſloop), 14 : Retaken by the Inconſtant, 36, T. F. Freemantle, in the Mediterranean, March ; having been captured from the Britiſh in June, 1794.

LE JEAN BART, 18 : Taken by the Cerberus, 32, J. Drew, and Sta Margaritta, 36, T. B. Martin, Channel, March 29. Afterwards in the Britiſh ſervice, named Arab, and loſt in June, 1796. — *See Britiſh ſhips loſt, &c.*

*LA GLOIRE, 40 : Taken by the Aſtrea, 32, Lord H. Powlett, deſpatched from the ſquadron of Rear-Admiral Colpoys, Channel, April 10, after a cloſe action of 58 minutes.

*LA GENTILLE, 40 : Taken by the Hannibal, 74, J. Markham, deſpatched from the ſquadron of Rear-Admiral Colpoys, Channel, April 11.

LE JEAN BART, 26 : Taken by the ſquadron under Sir J. B. Warren, off Rochfort, April 15. Afterwards in the Britiſh ſervice, and named *Laurel*.

L'EXPEDITION, (corvette,) 16 : Taken by Sir J. B. Warren's ſquadron, near Belle-Iſle, April 16.

GALATEA, 44 : Caſt away near the Penmarks, April 23.

*LA PREVOYANTE, armed en flute, 24, *(pierced for 40)* : ⎫ Taken by the Thetis, 38,
*LA RAISON, armed en flute,   18, *(pierced for 24)* : ⎭ Hon. A. F. Cochrane, and
                                                                                                          Huſſar,

Huffar, 28, J. P. Beresford, off the Chefapeake, May 17. (Three other fhips, in company with thefe, were engaged by the Thetis and Huffar, at the fame time, but made their efcape.)

COURIER NATIONALE, 18 : Taken by the Thorn, 16, R. W. Otway, after a gallant action of 35 minutes, in,the Weft Indies, May 25.

*L'ECLAIR,　　3 : ⎫ Taken by Sir R. J. Strachan's fquadron off the coaft of France,
*CRACHE FEU, 3 : ⎭ May 9.

LIBERTE', (corvette,) 20 : Sunk by the Alarm, 32, D. Milne, off Porto Rico, Weft Indies, May 30.

*LE TIGRE.　　　 80 : ⎫ Taken, after a long chafe, by the fleet under Admiral Lord
*ALEXANDER,　　74 : ⎬ Bridport, clofe in with Port l'Orient, June 23. Thefe
*LE FORMIDABLE. 74 : ⎭ fhips compofed part of a fleet confifting of twelve fhips of the line, eleven frigates, and fome fmaller veffels, more of which would doubtlefs have been taken, had they not been fheltered by the land.

*LA MINERVE, 42 : Taken by the Dido, 28, G. H. Towry, and Loweftoffe, 32, G. B. Middleton, after a very fpirited action of 3 hours ; in which they likewife engaged L'Artemife, 36, who fheered off, and efcaped by her fuperior failing.

*LA VESUVE, (G. V.) 4 : Taken by the Melampus, 36, Sir R. J. Strachan, and Hebe, 38. P. Minchin, near St. Maloes, July 3.

LA PERDRIX, 24 : Taken by the Vanguard, 74, S. Miller, near Antigua.

L'ALCIDE, 74 : Cut off from the rear of the French fleet, and ftruck to Admiral Hotham's fleet, in the Mediterranean, July 13, but, by accident, fhe caught fire, and blew up before poffeffion could be taken of her, and only 300 of the crew were faved.

L'ECHOUE', 28 : Run on-fhore and deftroyed on the Ifle of Rhé, by the Phaëton, 38, Hon. R. Stopford.

*LA VICTORIEUSE, (corvette,) 12 : ⎫ Taken by the fleet under Admiral Duncan, near
*LA SUFFISANTE, (corvette,)　14 : ⎭ the Texel, Auguft 25.

LA RESOLUE, (corvette,)　　10 : ⎫ Taken by the Agamemnon, 64, H. Nelfon, and
LA REPUBLIQUE, (G. B.)　　 6 : ⎬ the fquadron under his command, viz. Incon-
LA CONSTITUTION, (galley,) 5 : ⎨ ftant, 36, T. F. Freemantle ; Meleager, 32,
LA VIGILANTE, (galley,)　　5 : ⎭ G. Cockburn ; Southampton, 32, W. Shield ; Tartar, 28, ———— ; Ariadne, 20, R. Plampin ; and Speedy cutter, 14, Lieut. T. Elphinfton ; in the Bay of Alaffio, Mediterranean, Auguft 16.

L'ASSEMBLEE NATIONALE, 22 : Driven on the rocks of Triguier, by the Diamond, 38, Sir W. S Smith, knt. and loft with 20 of the crew.

LA RUDE, (G. V.) 12 : Burnt by La Pomone, 44, Sir J. B. Warren, bart. in Bourneaux-Bay, coaft of France, September 2.

VIGILANTE, (cutter,) 6 : Taken by the Childers, 14, R. Dacres, in the bay of St. Brieux, September 3.

SANS CULOTTES, 18 : Burnt by l'Aimable, 32, C. S. Davers, off Defeada, Weft Indies, September 22.

SUPERBE, 22 : Taken by the Vanguard, 74, S. Miller, in the Weft Indies, Sept. 30.

BRUTUS,

BRUTUS, 10: Taken by the Mermaid, 32, H. Warre, and Zebra, 16, N. Thompfon, off Grenada, October 10.

*REPUBLIQUAIN, 18: Taken by the Mermaid, 32, H. Warre, and Zebra, 16, N. Thompfon, in the Weft Indies, October 14.

L'EVEILLE, 18: Taken by the fquadron under Sir J. B. Warren, bart. off Rochfort, October 15.

PANDORA, 14: Taken by the Caroline, 36, W. Luke, in the North Sea, Dec. 1. Afterwards in the Britifh fervice, and loft in Nov. 1797. — *See Britifh fhips loft, &c.*

LES DROITS DU PEUPLE, 36: Loft off Drontheim, coaft of Norway, November.

1796.

*LA PERCANTE, (now *Jamaica*,) 26: Taken by the Intreoid, 64, Hon. C. Carpenter, off Porto Plata, Weft Indies, February.

LA FAVORITE, 22: Taken by the Alfred, 74, T. Drury, off Cape Finifterre, March.

*SARDINE, 22: ⎰ Taken by the Egmont, 74, J. Sutton, in company with the
*NEMESIS, 28: ⎱ Barfleur, 98, and others, near Tunis, March 9.
POSTILLON, (frigate,) ⎰

*LA BONNE CITOYENNE, 20: Taken by the Phaeton, 38, Hon. R. Stopford, near Cape Finifterre, March 10.

L'ETOURDIE, 16: Burnt by the Diamond, 38, Sir W. S. Smith, at Cape Frehel, Mar. 18.

MARSOUIN, 26: Taken by the Beaulieu, 44, L. Skynner, Weft Indies, March.

L'ETOILE, 30: Taken by Sir J. B. Warren's fquadron, near the Raz de Fontenay, coaft of France, March 20.

L'ALERTE, 14: Taken by the Sampfon, 64, J. Bingham, off St. Domingo.

*L'UNITE', 38: Taken by the Révolutionnaire, 44, F. Cole, defpatched from the fquadron under Sir Edward Pellew, off the coaft of France, April 13.

*LA ROBUSTE, (now *Scourge*,) 22: Taken by Sir J. B. Warren's fquadron, off the Saints, April 15.

*L'UNITE', (corvette,) (now *Surprife*,) 32: Taken by the Inconftant, 36, T. F. Fremantle, in the Mediterranean, April 20.

*LA VIRGINIE, 44: Taken by the Indefatigable, 44, Sir E. Pellew, and his fquadron, 40 leagues S.W. of the Lizard, April 22.

AURORE, 10: Taken by the Cleopatra, 32, C. Rowley, off the coaft of America, April.

L'ECUREUIL, (lugger-corvette,) 18: Set fire to and burnt by the barge and cutters of the Niger, 32, E. J. Foote, near the Penmarks, coaft of France, April 27.

L'ABEILLE, (cutter,) 14: Taken by the Dryad, 36, J. K. Pulling, off the Lizard, May 2.

LA VOLCAN, (brig-corvette,) 12, *(pierced for* 16): Taken by the Spencer, 18, A. F. Evans, off Bermuda, May 4, after a clofe action of one hour and a quarter.

LA

LA CIGNE, (cutter,) 14: Taken by the Doris, 36, Hon. C. Jones, off Scilly, May 7.
*L'ATHENIENE, (corvette,) 14: Taken by the Albicore, 16, R. Winthrop, near Barbadoes, May 8.
LA GENIE, (ketch,)   3 : ⎱ Taken by the fquadron under Commodore
LA NUMERO DOUZE, (G. B.)   1 : ⎰ H. Nelſon, at Oneglia, in the Mediterranean, May 31.
*THAMES, (now 32,) 36 : Captured from the Britiſh, Oct. 24, 1793. Retaken by the Santa Margaritta, 36, T. B. Martin, near Waterford, June 7. — *See Britiſh ſhips loſt, &c.*
LA TRIBUNE, 44 : Taken by the Unicorn, 32, T. Williams, off the coaſt of Ireland, June 7.
*LA PROSERPINE, (now *Amelia*,) 44 : Taken by the Dryad, 36, Lord A. Beauclerc, 40 leagues S.W. of Cape Clear, June 13.
₊ The Thames, La Tribune, and La Proſerpine, failed together from Breſt, accompanied by La Legere, 22. The two former and the latter had left Breſt but two days, when they were fallen in with by the Unicorn and Santa Margaritta, who inſtantly gave chafe (La Proſerpine having ſeparared in a fog the preceding evening). The Thames ſurrendered to the Santa Margaritta, after a cloſe attack, in leſs than 20 minutes ; but the ſmaller ſhip, Legere, made off to windward, and eſcaped. La Tribune, feeing her companion fall, made all fail ; the Unicorn then continued to chafe that ſhip, and kept on a running fight for 10 hours ; and, at half paſt 10 at night, after a purſuit of 210 miles, cloſe action commenced, which continued, with the greateſt heat, 35 minutes ; when, on the Unicorn's defeating a maſterly manœuvre of La Tribune, and completely diſmantling her, ſhe ſtruck, having 37 killed and 15 wounded, without a loſs to the Britiſh of one man. La Proſerpine was taken, as above-mentioned, by the Dryad, after a cloſe action of 45 minutes, and had 30 killed and 45 wounded. The Thames had 32 killed and 19 wounded. The total loſs of the Britiſh in the three ſhips was 4 killed and 10 or 12 wounded. His Majeſty was pleaſed, ſhortly after, to confer on Captain Williams the honour of knighthood. La Tribune, afterwards in the Britiſh ſervice, was loſt in Nov. 1797. — *See Britiſh ſhips loſt, &c.* (La Legere was captured on June 22, as hereafter-mentioned.)
L'UTILE, (corvette,) 24 : Boarded and taken by the Southampton, 32, J. Macnamara, near the Hieres Iſlands, Mediterranean, June 10.
LES TROIS COULEURS, (brig corvette,) 10 : ⎱ Taken by the Indefatigable, 44, Sir
LA BLONDE, (brig,)   16 : ⎰ E. Pellew. bart. and his fquadron, off Uſhant, June 11.
*LA LEGERE, (corvette,) (now 24,) 22 : Taken by the Apollo, 36, J. Manley, and Doris, 36, Hon. C. Jones, to the S.W. of Scilly, June 22.
*LA RENOMMÉE, 44 : Taken by the Alfred, 74, T. Drury, off St. Domingo, July 12.
L'ALERTE, 16 : Taken by the Carysfort, 28, J. Alexander, Eaſt Indies, Auguſt 19.
L'ANDROMACHE, 44 : Run on-ſhore and burnt near Arcaſſon, coaſt of France, by the ſquadron under Sir J. B. Warren, bart. Auguſt 22.

L'ELIZA-

L. ELIZABETH, 36 : Taken by the fquadron under Vice-Admiral G. Murray, Halifax ftation, Auguft 28.

L'ELIZA, (fchooner,) 10 : Taken by the Fury, 16, H. Evans, Weft Indies, October 18.

LA CERF VOLANT, (corvette,) 18 : Taken by the Magicienne, 32, H. Ricketts, off St. Domingo, Nov. 1.

L'ETONNANT, (corvette,) 18 : Driven on-fhore and deftroyed by the Minerva, 44, G. Cockburn, and Melampus, 36, G. Moore, at the entrance of Barfleur-Harbour, Nov. 13.

*L'ETNA, (now *Cormorant*, 20,) 18 : Taken by the Melampus, 36, G. Moore, and Childers, 14, S. Poyntz, off the coaft of France, November 13.

LA DECIUS, 28 : ⎫ Engaged together by the Lapwing, 28, R. Barton, near
LA VAILLANT, (brig,) 4 : ⎭ St. Martin's, Weft Indies, Nov. 27. · After a clofe action of an hour, La Vailiant, which carried 32 and 24 pounders, bore away, and in half an hour after La Décius ftruck. The brig, which was full of. troops, ran on-fhore on St. Martin's, and was deftroyed by the fire of the Lapwing. On the following day, Captain Barton, being chafed by two large French frigates, found it neceffary to fet fire to La Décius, to prevent her falling into their hands. La Décius, being full of troops, had 80 killed and 40 wounded. The Lapwing had but 1 killed and 6 wounded.

L'AFRICAINE, 18 : Taken by the Quebec, 32, J. Cook, off St. Domingo. Dec. 3.

LA GENERAL LEVEAU, (brig,) 16 : Taken by the Refource, 28, F. Watkins, and Mermaid, 32, R. W. Otway, off St. Domingo, December 10.

SEDUISANT, 74 : Loft on the rocks called the Saints, near Breft, December 16.

SCÆVOLA, 40 : Foundered off the coaft of Ireland, December 30.

L'IMPATIENTE, 44 : Went on-fhore and was loft near Crookhaven, Ireland, December 30, with 565 troops and feamen : only 7 men faved. — *This fhip, in the Gazette account, is ftated to have carried but 20 guns.*

LA JUSTINE, (S. S.) 44 : Loft off the coaft of Ireland, December.

L'AMANRANTHE, (floop,) 14 : Taken by the Diamond, 38, Sir R. J. Strachan, off Alderney, December 31. Afterwards in the Britifh fervice, and loft September, 1799. — *See Britifh fhips loft, &c.*

LA VESTALE, 44 : Taken by the Terpfichore, 32, R. Bowen, near Cadiz, December 13 ; but retaken next day.

1797.

*LA TORTUE, (now *L'Uranie*, 38,) 44 : Taken, with troops, by the Polyphemus, 64, G. Lumfdaine, off the coaft of Ireland, January 5.

SURVEILLANTE, 44 : Captured and fcuttled in Bantry-Bay, Ireland, January.

LA VILLE DE L'ORIENT, (Armed en flute,) 36 : Taken, with 400 huffars, &c. by the Unicorn, 32, Sir T. Williams, knt.; Doris, 36, Hon. C. Jones; and Druid, 32, E. Codrington ; coaft of Ireland, January 7.

SUFFREIN, (S. S.) 44 : Sunk by the Dædalus, 32, G. Countefs, Majeftic, 74, G. B. Weftcott, and Incendiary, 14, G. Barker, off Ufhant, January 8.

*L'ATALANTE,

*L'ATALANTE, (floop,) 16 : Taken by the Phœbe, 36, R. Barlow, 18 leagues S. W. of Scilly, January 10.

L ALLÉGREE, (store-ship,) 200 tons, laden with ammunition, &c. : Taken by the Spitfire, 16, M. Seymour, off Uthant, January 12.

LES DROITS DE L HOMME, 74 : Run aground near the Penmarks, and loft, with 170 of her men, after a fevere running-engagement, of 16 hours and a half, with the Indefatigable, 44, Sir E Pellew, and Amazon, 36, R. C. Reynolds, in the night of January 13.

A SCHOONER, (name unknown,) 2 : Taken,by the Matilda, 28, H. Mitford, off Barbadoes, February 13.

T *LA RESISTANCE, (now ⎤ Taken by the St. Fiorenzo, 44, Sir H. Neale, bart. and La
  Fifgard, 44,)   48 : ⎬   Nymphe, 36, J. Cooke, off Breft, March 9, without ha-
*LA CONSTANCE, 24 : ⎦   ving one man killed or wounded.   Thefe were the ships which, in company with La Vengeance, 48, landed the French convicts, under the difguife of foldiers, in Wales.

LA MODESTE, 20 : Taken by the Fox, 32, P. Malcolm, off Vizagapatnam in the E. Indies.

L'HARMONIE, 44 : Run on-shore and destroyed, at St. Domingo, by the Thunderer, 74, W. Ogilvy and Valiant, 74, E. Crawley, April 17.

*LA JALOUSE, (corvette,) 18 : Taken by the Veftal, 28, C. White, in the North Sea, May 13.

*LA MUTINE, (corvette,) 14 : Boarded and cut out of the Bay of Santa Cruz, Teneriffe, by the boats of the Lively, 36, B. Hallowell, and Minerve, 42, G. Cockburn, commanded by Lieut. T. M. Hardy of La Minerve, under a heavy fire from every part of the bay.

LA HARRIOTT, 6 : Taken by L'Aigle, 32, C. Tyler, near Lifbon, June 12.

LA CALLIOPE, 36 : Destroyed by Sir J. B. Warren's fquadron, on the coaft of France, July 17.

LA FREEDOM, (armed en flute,) 8 : Taken and burnt by Sir J. B. Warren's fquadron, July 17.

A SHIP CORVETTE, (name unknown,) 22 : Taken and bilged, by Sir J. B. Warren's fquadron, on the coaft of France, Auguft 11.

A BRIG, (G. V.) 12 : Taken and funk by Sir J. B. Warren's fquadron, Auguft 11.

*LA GAIETE', (corvette,) 20 : Taken by the Arethufa, 38, T. Wolley, 125 leagues E. by S. of Bermuda, Auguft 20.

L'EGALITE', (chaffe-marée,) 8 : Taken by Sir J. B. Warren's fquadron, on the coaft of France, Auguft 23.

LE PETIT DIABLE. (cutter,) 18 : Taken and bilged by Sir J. B. Warren's fquadron, on the coaft of France, Auguft 27.

*L'ESPOIR, (corvette,) 16 : Taken by the Thalia, 36, Lord H. Powlett, Mediterranean, September 10.

LA DECOUVERTE, 18 : Taken by the Unité, 36, B. Rowley, Channel, Oct. 9.

*LE RANGER, (corvette, *now Le Venturier,)* 14: Taken by the Indefatigable, 44, Sir E. Pellew, bart. near Teneriffe, October 14. — Retaken ; and again captured by the Galatea, 32, G. Byng, November 6.   C   *L'EPER-

*L'EPERVIER, 16 : Taken by the Cerberus, 32, J. Drew, Irish station, Nov. 12.

LA MEDUSE, 44 : Burnt by her confort, L'Infurgente, on her return from America, in November, having been rendered unserviceable by rough weather.

*LA NEREIDE, 36 : Taken by the Phœbe, 36, R. Barlow, after a smart engagement of two hours, in which La Nereide had 20 men killed and 55 wounded, off Scilly, December 22. The Phœbe had 3 killed and 10 wounded.

*DAPHNE, (corvette, 30,) *now* 20 : Captured from the Britifh, February 12, 1795. *See Britifh fhips loft, &c.* Retaken by the Anfon, 44, P. C. Durham, in the Bay of Bifcay, December 28.

LA REPUBLIQUE TRIOMPHANTE, (corvette,) 14 : Taken by the Severn, 44, T. Boys, and Pelican, 18, J. Gafcoyne, in the Weft Indies, December.

1798.

LA CHERI, 26 : Taken by La Pomone, 44, R. C. Reynolds, in the Bay of Bifcay, January 5, and foundered fhortly after.

LA DESIREE, (fchooner,) 6 : Boarded and taken by the boats of La Babet, 20, J. Mainwaring, manned with 24 feamen, under the command of Lieut. S. Pym, 3 leagues from the fhip, after rowing for 4 hours, between Martinique and Dominica, January 16. The enemy made a defperate refiftance, and had 46 men, of whom 3 were killed and 15 wounded. The Britifh had 1 feaman killed and 5 wounded.

LE SCIPION, 20 : Taken by the Alfred, 74, T. Totty, under the batteries of Baffe Terre, Guadaloupe, Feb. 16.

LA SOURIS, (chaffe-marée,) 16 : Taken by the Badger, (G. V.) 4, Lieut. C. P. Price, and Sandfly, (G. V.) Lieut. R. Bourne, near the Ifles of St. Marcou, Channel, Feb. 26.

LE QUARTORZE JUILLET, 74 : Bürnt by accident at L'Orient, May 1.

LA SAINTE FAMILLE (chaffe-marée) : Taken by L'Impétueux, 78, J. W. Payne, and Sylph, 16, J. C. White, April 5.

L'ARROGANTE, (G. V.) 6 : Taken by the Jafon, 36, C. Stirling, near Breft, April 19.

*L'HERCULE, 74 : Taken by the Mars, 74, Alexander Hood, after a very fevere conteft of one hour and a half, at the entrance of the Paffage du Raz, near Breft, April 21, in which the Britifh had 90 perfons killed and wounded. " No praife can add one ray of brilliancy" to the diftinguifhed name of Capt. Hood for his brave conduct in this action ; he died of a wound he received in fupporting it, juft as L'Hercule ftruck.

A CORVETTE, (name unknown,) 22 : Taken by the Caroline, 36, W. Luke, near Lifbon. *This corvette is fince fuppofed to have been a privateer.*

FLIBUSTIER (G. V.) : Taken, and feveral others funk, by the batteries of the iflands of St. Marcou, in the Channel, commanded by Lieut. C. P. Price of the Badger, (D. H.) and Lieut. R. Bourne of the Sandfly, (G. V.) May 7, in an attack made by a very confiderable flotilla againft thofe iflands, which was gallantly and completely defeated. The Adamant, 50, Eurydice, 28, and Oreftes, 16, were on that ftation, but not in a fituation to afford material affiftance.

LA

LA MONDOVI, 16 : Cut out of Cerigo, Mediterranean, in the moft gallant manner, under a very heavy fire, by the boats of the Flora, 36, A. Wilfon, commanded by Lieut. J. Ruffell, May 13.

A NUMBER OF BOATS, with the locks and bafon-gates of the canal from Oftend to Bruges : The boats were burnt, and the bafon-gates blown up and deftroyed, by a naval and military force, under command of Capt. Home Popham, of the Expedition, 44, and Major General Coote, May 19.

LA CONFIANTE, 36 : Run on-fhore and burnt near Havre, by the Hydra, 36, Sir F. Laforey ; Trial, (cutter,) 12, Lieut. H. Garrett ; and Vefuvius, (Bb,),8, D. Facey ; May 31.

LA CORCYRE, 16 : Taken by the Flora, 32, R. G. Middleton, off Sicily, June 22.

EGALITE', 20 : Run on-fhore and deftroyed by the Aurora, 28, H. Digby, near Cape Machichicao, Bay of Bifcay, June 22.

*LA SENSIBLE, 36 : Taken, with General Baraguay D'Hilliers and his fuite, on return-ing from Malta, by the Sea-Horfe, 36, E. I. Foote, after a chafe of 12 hours and a clofe ac-tion of 8 minutes, in which La Senfible had 18 killed and 36 wounded, including the Cap-tain.   The Sea-Horfe had 2 killed and 16 wounded.

*LA SEINE, 42: Taken, after a moft brave and exemplary refiftance, in an action which continued from 11 at night until half paft two in the morning, by the Jafon, 36, C. Stirling, and La Pique, 36, D. Milne, in the Paffage-Breton, Coaft of France, June 30.   She was brought to action by La Pique, in a running-fight, until the Jafon run between, and received the fire of the enemy.   The paffage was fo fhoal, that the fhips grounded, and La Pique un-fortunately bilged, fo that it was neceffary fubfequently to deftroy her.   See Britifh fhips loft, &c.   La Seine had 170 men killed and 100 badly wounded ; the Jafon 7 killed and 12 wounded, including Capt. Stirling among the latter ; and La Pique had 1 killed and 7 wounded.   The Mermaid, 32, J. N. Newman, had joined in chafe, but could not get up in time to have a fhare in the action.

TAKEN.		Taken, burnt, and funk, by the fquadron under the
*LE FRANKLIN, *(now Canopus,)*	80 :	command of Rear-Admiral Sir Horatio Nelfon, K. B. off the Bay of Shoals or Bequier, near the
*LE TONNANT,	80 :	Mouth of the Nile, Auguft 1 and 2. The fhips
LE GUERRIER,	74 :	compofing the French fleet, commanded by Ad-
*LE SPARTIATE,	74 :	miral Brueys, were moored, with fprings on
*LE CONQUERANT,	74 :	their cables, in a ftrong line of battle for defend-
*L'AQUILON, *(now Aboukir,)*	74 :	ing the entrance of the bay, with their heads to
L'HEUREUX,	74 :	the N. W. flanked by numerous gun-boats, four,
LE MERCURE,	74 :	frigates, and a battery of guns and mortars on
LE SOUVERAIN PEUPLE,	74 :	Bequier-Ifland, an ifland in their van, between which ifland and their van-fhip was a diftance of
		about one mile and a quarter. Their rear was
BURNT.		protected to leeward by a fhoal, having only 3
L'ORIENT,	120 :	

LE TIMOLEON, 74: ⎫ or 4 fathoms of water on it ; and their ships were moored at
L'ARTEMISE, 36: ⎬ two-thirds of a cable's length from each other.
    SUNK.   ⎪ The Britiſh ſquadron, under the command of Rear-Admiral
LA SERIEUSE, 36: ⎭ Nelſon, approached this poſition of the French fleet in the
morning of the 1ſt of Auguſt, 1798, from the weſtward. The
action commenced at ſun-ſet of the ſame day, in purſuance of the admiral's ſignal to engage
from van to the centre, *both to windward and leeward.* In going down, (the wind being at
N. W.) the ſquadron were annoyed in ſome degree by the battery, gun-boats, and the French
line, which fired on them as they ran down. The Culloden, Alexander, and Swiftſure, had
been detained with a ſmall prize, and followed in about one hour and a half afterwards: In
doing this, the Culloden grounded on the northern ſhoal of Bequier-Iſland, nor was ſhe able
to be gotten off in time to participate in the dangers and honours of the day. The Mutine
brig remained to aſſiſt her. This miſchance, however, ſerved to point out the danger to the
Alexander and Swiftſure, which, conſequently avoiding it, got into their reſpective ſta-
tions.

The action was continued from about ſix o'clock in the evening of the 1ſt of Auguſt till
near three in the morning of the 2d. It was then intermitted for about two hours, and was
afterwards continued till about two in the afternoon of the 2d. The rear of the French fleet
was not in action for ſeveral hours after its commencement. L'Orient, the flag-ſhip of Admiral Brueys, took fire about 10 o'clock in the night of the 1ſt, and ſhortly after blew up,
the admiral, and Caſa Bianca, his captain, having been previouſly killed, and her crew de-
ſtroyed by this event. The fate of the other ſhips is ſubjoined to this narrative, by which it
will be ſeen that their two rear ſhips of the line and two frigates only eſcaped the general
overthrow. Nor could the Britiſh admiral prevent their flight, as he had no ſhip in a condition to ſupport the Zealous, Capt. Hood, who endeavoured to perform this ſervice. Capt.
Weſtcott, of the Majeſtic, was killed early in the action; but her firſt lieutenant, R. Cuth-
bert, ſo ably conducted her afterwards, as to receive the honour of public mention in the admiral's official communication! Indeed, to the judgement and valour of all the officers, and
to the courage of the crews, does the Britiſh admiral aſcribe the ſucceſs of this important day;
but, with the modeſty of true courage, he omits to mention his own judicious mode of the
attack, leaving to others the appreciation of its merits. He was himſelf wounded in the
head, and obliged to be carried off the deck ; thence the command of his ſhip devolved on
Capt. Edward Berry, who was fully equal to the duty, and who received his juſt commen-
dation.

The following are the names of the ſhips compoſing the Britiſh ſquadron and French fleet,
with their guns and men, and the number of Britiſh killed and wounded :

BRITISH

BRITISH SQUADRON.

Ships and Guns.		Men	Captains.			K.	W.
Culloden —	—	74	590	T. Trowbridge —	—	—	—
Thefeus —	—	74	590	R. W. Miller —	—	5	30
Alexander —	—	74	590	A. J. Ball —	—	14	58
Vanguard —	—	74	595	Rr-Ad. Sir H. Nelfon, K. B. / Capt. E. Berry	—	30	75
Minotaur —	—	74	640	T. Louis —	—	23	64
Leander —	—	50	343	T. B. Thompfon —	—	—	14
Swiftfure —	—	74	590	B. Hallowell —	—	7	22
Audacious —	—	74	590	D. Gould —	—	1	35
Defence —	—	74	590	J. Peyton —	—	4	11
Zealous —	—	74	590	S. Hood —	—	1	7
Orion —	—	74	590	Sir J. Saumarez —	—	13	29
Goliah —	—	74	590	T. Foley —	—	21	41
Majeftic —	—	74	590	G. B. Weftcott —	—	50	143
Bellerophon —	—	74	590	H. D'E. Darby —	—	49	148
La Mutine (brig) —	—	14	110	T. M. Hardy —	—	—	—

TOTAL 1026 8178   TOTAL 218 677

FRENCH FLEET.

Ships and Guns.			Men.	
Le Guerrier	—	74	600	(The van-fhip) taken.
Le Conquérant	—	74	700	Taken.
Le Spartiate	—	74	700	Taken.
L'Aquilon	—	74	700	Taken.
Le Souverain Peuple,		74	700	Taken.
Le Franklin	—	80	800	Rear-Adm. Blanquet. Taken.
L'Orient	—	120	1010	Admiral Brueys. Burnt.
Le Tonant	—	80	800	Taken.
L'Heureux	—	74	700	Taken.
Le Timoléon	—	74	700	Burnt.
Le Mercure	—	74	700	Taken.
Le Guillaume Tell,		80	800	2d Rear-Ad. Villeneuve.
Le Généreux	—	74	700	Efcaped. [Efcaped.
La Diane —	—	48	300	Efcaped.
La Juftice	—	34	300	Efcaped.
L'Artemife	—	36	250	Burnt.
La Sérieufe	—	36	250	Sunk.

1190   10710   C 3   Although

Although Le Généreux and Le Guillaume Tell efcaped hence, they were afterwards captured as mentioned hereafter, the former on February 18, and the latter on March 30, 1800.

For their meritorious conduct in this engagement, Rear-Admiral Nelfon, his officers, and feamen, received the thanks of both Houfes of Parliament. His Majefty was pleafed alfo to confer on the rear-admiral the dignity of a Baron of Great Britain, with a penfion of £3000 per annum for his fervices. Captains E. Berry and T. B. Thompfon, for their very diftinguifhed conduct, received the honour of knighthood. Gold medals were likewife prefented to the captains of all the fhips of the line as to thofe in the engagement with Earl Howe on June 1, 1794. And the Grand Signior, immediately upon receiving the news of the victory, tranfmitted to Sir H. Nelfon, by a Turkifh frigate, a fuperb diamond aigrette, called a *Chelengh*, or plume of triumph, taken from one of the Imperial turbans, with a pelice of fable fur of the firft quality, and a purfe of 2000 fequins, to be diftributed among the wounded feamen.

L'AVENTURIERE, (corvette,) 12 : Cut out in the night of Auguft 3, from the port of Corigiou, near the ifle of Bas, and brought off, under a heavy and long-continued fire from the batteries, by the boats of the Melpomene, 44, Sir Charles Hamilton; and Childers, 14, J. O Bryan, under the command of Lieut. Shortland.

LA VAILLANTE, (corvette,) 20 : Taken by the Indefatigable, 44, Sir E. Pellew, bart. in the Bay of Bifcay, Auguft 7. Afterwards in the Britifh fervice, named the Danaë, and retaken by mutiny, March 17, 1800. *See Britifh fhips loft, &c.*

LIGURIA, *(Genoefe,)* 26 : Taken by L'Efpoir, 16, L. O. Bland, in the Mediterranean, Auguft 7, after a very gallant and obftinate action of near 4 hours. The Liguria, befides her great fuperiority in larger guns, had 12 long-wall pieces and 4 fwivels. Of her crew, 120 in number, 7 were killed and 14 wounded; including the captain among the latter. L'Efpoir had 1 killed and 2 wounded.

*LA FORTUNE, (corvette,) 18 : Taken by the Swiftfure, 74, B. Hallowell, off the Nile, Auguft 11.

LA NEPTUNE, 20 : Taken, with 270 troop, by the Hazard, 16, W. Butterfield, after an action of 1 hour and 50 minutes off the coaft of Ireland, Auguft 12.

*LA LEGERE, (G.V.) 6 : Taken by the Alcmene, 32, G. Hope; off Alexandria, Auguft 22.

*LA DECADE, 36 : Taken by the Magnanime, 44, Hon. M. De Courcy, and Naiad, 38. W. Pierrepont, off Cape Finifterre, Auguft 24.

*TORRIDE, (ketch,) 7 : Taken by the boats of the Goliath, 74, T. Foley, commanded by Lieut. W. Debufk, from under the guns of the Caftle of Bequier, near the Nile, Auguft 25.

LA REUNION, (brig corvette,) 6 : Taken by L'Oifeau, 36, C. Brifbane, Eaft Indies, September 1.

L'ANEMONE, (G.V.) 4 : Deftroyed at Damietta, on the Nile, by the Sea-Horfe, 38, E. I. Foote, and Emerald, 36, T. M. Waller, September 2.

LA

LA FLORE, 36 : Taken by the Phaeton, 38, Hon. R. Stopford, and Anfon, 44, P. C. Durham, Channel ftation, September 6.

*LE HOCHE, *(now Donegal,)*   80: ⎫ With troops for the invafion of Ireland. Taken
*L'AMBUSCADE,   40: ⎪ by the fquadron under Sir John Borlafe Warren,
LA COQUILLE,   40: ⎪ bart. off the N. W. coaft of Ireland, October
*LA BELLONE, *(now Proferpine,)* 36: ⎬ 12, 13, and 18. The Britifh fquadron con-
*LA RESOLUE, (now 36,)   40: ⎪ fifted of the Canada, 74, Sir J. B. Warren,
*LA LOIRE,   46: ⎭ bart.; Robuft, 74, E. Thornbrough; Fou-
droyant, 80, Sir T. Byard; Magnanime, 44, Hon. M. De Courcy ; Anfon, 44, P. C. Dur-
ham ; Ethalion, 38, G. Countefs ; Melampus, 36, G. Moore ; and Amelia, 44, Hon. C.
Herbert. The French fquadron confifted of the fhips here enumerated, with L'Immortalité,
42 ; La Romaine, 40 ; La Semillante, 36 ; and La Biche, (fchooner,) 8.

On the 11th October, at noon, the French fquadron was feen to windward, by the Amelia,
in the N. E. when the Canada made fignal for a general chafe. At 4 P. M. one fhip was
feen from the deck of the Melampus ; at 15 minutes paft 5, Canada made rendezvous-fignal
for Lough-Swilly. The fquadron kept their wind all night, which was very fqually, and
the Melampus, at about 10 o'clock, fpoke the Anfon, who had unfortunately carried away
her mizen-maft. At 5 A. M. on the 12th, being moderate weather, the French fquadron
was feen about half a league to windward in the N. E. Signal made to tack and prepare
for battle. One of the enemy's fhips (Le Hoche) had loft her main-topmaft. At 6, the Robuft and Magnanime commenced action with Le Hoche, by fignal from the Canada. While
thefe fhips were thus engaged, the Canada, endeavouring to get to windward, tacked, and,
paffing the enemy's line of frigates to windward, joined in tne engagement with Le Hoche,
which foon after, at 9 o'clock, ftruck, and was boarded by Robuft, by fignal from the Canada. The Melampus, as fhe was beating to windward, fired at Le Hoche, and then ftood
on for L'Ambufcade, which, after half an hour's engagement, ftruck to the Melampus, at about
11 o clock ; the Foudroyant, however, having, from to leeward, fired bow-guns at her.
L'Ambufcade, dropping a-ftern, was taken poffeffion of by the Magnanime, in purfuance of
a fignal from the Canada, The Canada, Foudroyant, Ethalion, Melampus, and Amelia,
then chafed the remaining fhips making off to the W. S. W. After an hour's chafe, La Coquille alfo ftruck to the fquadron, and was left for the Magnanime to take poffeffion of, by
fignal from the Canada. At half paft 12 o'clock, the Melampus was engaging La Bellone ;
but the Ethalion coming up, and having paffed to windward, by fignal, (and getting between
them, to windward of the Melampus,) engaged her clofe on-board for three quarters of an
hour, when fheiftruck to the Ethalion. The chafe of the remaining five fhips was continued ;
but, night coming on, they were loft fight of. At the time of their flight, the Anfon fuf-
tained a fevere fire from them, which fhe gallantly returned ; but, from the lofs of her mizen-
maft, was obliged to drop a-ftern. Thus were Le Hoche, L'Ambufcade, La Coquille, and
La Bellone, the conquefts of the 12th October. On the 13th, the Melampus was ordered,
by Sir J. B. Warren, to go into St. John's Bay, in fearch of a frigate which the fquadron
had chafed in there the night before. In confequence of which, at half paft ten, P. M. of
the

the 13th, the Melampas faw 2 fail to windward (La Réfolue and L'Immortalité). At half paft 11, P. M. got up clofe a-beam of La Réfolue, and in 20 minutes gave her 5 broadfides, which fhe did not return with a fingle gun; fhe was then boarded and taken poffeffion of; her confort, L'Immortalité, having given her no affiftance. The Mermaid, 32, J. Newman, afterwards fell in with La Loire, whom fhe engaged and crippled, but was herfelf fo difabled as not to purfue the conteft; but, on the 18th, the Anfon, 44, P. C. Durham, having been joined by Kanguroo, (brig,) 18, E. Brace, fell in with, engaged, and took, La Loire, off Cape Clear, after an action of one hour and a quarter, which was moft gallantly difputed, and in which La Loire had 48 men killed and 75 wounded. L'Immortalité was taken on the 20th October by the Fifgard as hereafter mentioned. La Romaine, La Semillante, and La Biche, efcaped.

For their conduct in thefe actions, fo important in their confequence, Commodore Sir J. B. Warren, his officers, and feamen, received the thanks of both Houfes of Parliament.

*L'IMMORTALITE', (now 36,) 42: Taken by the Fifgard, 38, T. B. Martin, on her return to Breft, and within a few leagues of that port, October 20, after a long and well-fought action, in which the enemy had 44 killed, including the captain, and 61 wounded. The Britifh had 10 killed and 26 wounded.

*LA FULMINANTE, (cutter,) 8: Taken by L'Efpoir, 76, L. O. Bland, Mediterranean, October 29.

LA FOUINE, (lugger,) 8: Taken by the Sylph, 16, J. C. White, near Breft, November 17.

L'HIRONDELLE, (corvette,) 20: Taken by the Phaëton, 38, Hon. R. Stopford; Ambufcade, 32, H. Jenkins; and Stag, 32, J. S. Yorke; Channel ftation, November 20.

LA WILDING, (A. T.) 14: Taken by the Spitfire, 20, M. Seymour, in the Bay of Bifcay, December 28.

1799.

*LA FORTE, 50: Taken by La Sybille, 44, Edward Cooke, off the Sand-Heads of Bengal River, Eaft Indies, February 28, after a well-fought action of one hour and 40 minutes, in which the enemy was totally difmafted. The gallant Captain Cooke, who difplayed the greateft degree of courage, prefence of mind, and profeffional abilities, was mortally wounded, and died fhortly after.

LA PRUDENTE, (pierced for 42,) 30: Taken by the Dædalus, 32, H. L. Ball, after an action of 57 minutes, Cape of Good Hope ftation, February 9.

L'HIRONDELLE, (brig corvette,) 16: Taken by the Telegraph, (hired brig,) 16, Lieut. J. Worth, 9 leagues N.W. from the Ifle of Bas, coaft of France, March 18, after a clofe action of 3 hours and a half.

MARIANNE.	4:	Taken, with a battering train of artillery, ammunition,
LA NEGRESSE,	6:	platforms, &c. deftined for the fiege of Acre, by the
LA FOUDRE,	8:	guard-boats, &c. of Le Tigre, 80, Commodore Sir

LA.

LA DANGEREUSE,   6 : ⎫   W. S. Smith, off Cape Carmel, Mediterranean, March
LA MARIA ROSE,   4 : ⎪   18. La Torride had been captured by the French
LA DAME DE GRACE,   4 : ⎬   flotilla on the fame day.
LES DEUX FRERES,   4 : ⎪
LA TORRIDE,   2 : ⎭
COURIER, (corvette,) 16 : Taken by the Zealous, 74, S. Hood, Mediterranean.
LA SANS QUARTIER, (lugger,) 14 : Taken by the Danaë, 20, Lord Proby, off the
Ifles Chofey, coaft of France, April 9.
N. B. *La Créole, 48, formerly ftated to have been wrecked at Nantz, was afterwards re-
fitted.*
LA REBECCA, (chaffe-marée,) 16 : Taken by the Black Joke,, (now Suwarrow,)
(fchooner,) 10, Lieut. J. Nicolfon, 20 leagues weft of Ufhant, April·27.
A CORVETTE, (name unknown,) 16 : Taken by the Lion, 64, M. Dixon, Mediterra-
nean, April.
LA JUNON,
 (now *Princefs Charlotte*,)   40 : ⎫ Taken by a detachment from the fquadron under the
*L'ALCESTE,   36 : ⎪ command of Vice-Admiral Lord Keith, confifting
*COURAGEUX,   32 : ⎬ of the Centaur, 74, J. Markham ; Bellona, 74, Sir
*LA SALAMINE, (brig,)   ⎪ T. B. Thompfon ; Captain, 74, Sir R. J. Strachan;
 (now 16,)   18 : ⎬ Emerald, 36, T. M. Waller ; and Santa Terefa, 42,
*L ALERTE, (brig,)   ⎪ G. Barker ; Mediterranean, June 18.
 (now *Minorca*,)   14 : ⎭
A SHIP, (name unknown,) 24 : Blown up in engaging the Trincomalee, (floop,) 16,
J. Rowe, at the entrance of the Straits of Babelmandel, by which both fhips· perifhed,
October. — *See Britifh fhips loft, &c.*
LA VESTALE, 36 : Taken by the Clyde, 36, C. Cunningham, off the mouth of the
river Garonne or Bourdeaux, Auguft 20.
*L'HUSSAR, (corvette,) (now *Surinam*,) 20 : Taken at Surinam by the fquadron under
Vice-Admiral Lord Hugh Seymour, Auguft 20.
REPUBLICAINE, 32 : Taken by the Tamer, 32, T. Weftern, off Surinam, Auguft 26.
LE ST. JACQUES, (lugger,) 6 : Taken by the Triton, 32, J. Gore, off L'Orient,
September 13.
*L'ARETHUSE, (brig corvette,) (now *Raven*,) 18 : Taken by the Excellent, 74, Hon.
R. Stopford, near L'Orient, October 10.
LA CHARENTE, 44 : Loft on entering L'Orient, after having conveyed the banifhed
deputies to Cayenne, November 10.
L'EGYPTIENNE, (pierced for 44,) 18 : ⎫ Taken by the Solebay, 32, S. Poyntz, on the
*L'ECLAIR, (now *Nimroa*,)   16 : ⎪ coaft of St. Domingo, Nov. 22. La Ven-
LA SARIER, (brig,)   12 : ⎬ geur, formerly the Charlotte, 10, had been
LA VENGEUR, (fchooner.)   8 : ⎭ captured from the Britifh. — *See Britifh fhips
loft, &c.*

                                                                                        LA

22   FRENCH NATIONAL SHIPS'

LA SURPRISE (corvette): Taken by the Braave, 40, T. Alexander, in the East Indies.

LA PRENEUSE, 44: Run on-shore near Port Louis, Isle of France, by the Tremendous, 74, J. Osborn, and Adamant, 50, W. Hotham, and destroyed by the boats of those ships under Lieut. Gray, of the Adamant, December 11.

1800.

LA BRUILLE GUILLI, (corvette,) 20 : Lost on a rock in Brest road, and only 38 of the crew saved, January 7.

*LA PALLAS, (now La Pique,) 40 : Taken by La Loire, 46, J. N. Newman ; Danaë, 20, Lord Proby ; Fairy, 16, J. S. Horton ; Harpy, 18, H. Bazely ; and Raileur, 20, W. J. Turquand ; under the Seven Islands, coast of France, February 6, after being crippled over night by the Fairy and Harpy.

*LA VIDETTE, (corvette,) 14 : Taken by the Triton, 32, J. Gore, near the Black Rocks, coast of France, February 10.

NOMBRE 57, (gun-vessel,) 1 : Taken by the Aristocrat, (brig,) 18, Lieut. C. J. D'Auvergne, off Cape Frehel, February 19.

*LE GENEREUX,   74 : ⎫ Taken, with Admiral Perrée, by Rear-
LA VILLE DE MARSEILLES, (S. S.)   ⎬ Admiral Lord Nelson's squadron, in
(since lost.)   ⎭ the Mediterranean, February 18.

A GENOESE POLACRE, (name unknown,) 14 : Driven on-shore, and destroyed, off Narbonne, in the Mediterranean, by the Pearl, 32, S. Ballard, February 9.

LA LIGURIENNE, (brig,) 16 (built with screw-bolts) : Taken, by the Peterell, (sloop,) 16, F. W. Austen, within point-blank shot of two batteries, after a well-contested action of more than an hour and a half, and after having driven off a corvette of the same force, and a xebec, in the bay of Marseilles, March 21. The Mermaid, 32, R. D. Oliver, being in sight to leeward, but so situated as not to afford material assistance.

*LE GUILLAUME TELL, (now Malta,) 84: Taken by the Lion, 64, M. Dixon ; Foudroyant, 80, Sir Edward Berry ; and Penelope, 36, H. Blackwood ; in the Mediterranean, March 30.

NEPTUNE, (schooner,) 4: Taken, with General Des Fourneaux, by the Mayflower Pr. James Le Blair, on a cruise off the coast of France, April.

DRAGON, (brig corvette,) 14: Taken by the Cambrian, 40, Hon. A. K. Legge, and Fisgard, 44, T. B. Martin, in the Channel, May 5.

LA PRIMA, (galley of 50 oars,) 2: Taken by a detachment of ships' boats, under Capt. Philip Beaver, at Genoa, May 20.

LA LEGERE, (lugger,) 3: Taken by the Netley, (schooner,) 16, Lieut. F. G. Bond, in the Mediterranean, May 31.

LA CRUELLE, (brig,) 16: Taken by the Mermaid, 32, R. D. Oliver, near Toulon, June 1.

L'INSO-

L'INSOLENTE, (brig corvette,) 18 : Burnt, with feveral fmall craft, by gun-launches and boats, under Lieut. J. Pilfold, of L'Impétueux, 78, Sir Edward Pellew, in the Morbihan, June 6.

LA CERBERE, (gun-brig, 87 men,) 7 : Cut out from under the batteries of Port Louis, by acting Lieut. J. Coghlan, (of the Viper cutter,) in a ten-oared cutter, belonging to L'Impétueux, 78, with only 20 men, July 29.   Lieut. Coghlan and 7 men were wounded, and 1 killed.   Of the enemy, 6 were killed and 20 wounded.   The prize was given up by the fquadron, to mark their admiration of the bravery exhibited in its capture.

DILIGENTE, (corvette,) 12 : Taken by the Crefcent, 36, W. G. Lobb, on the Jamaica ftation, June.

LA REVANCHE, 4 : Taken by the Phœnix, 36, L. W. Halfted, near the Hieres Iflands, Mediterranean, June 17.

LA DIANE, 42 : Taken by the Northumberland, 74, G. Martin ; Succefs, 32, S. Peard ; and Généreux, 74, M. Dixon ; in endeavouring to efcape from Malta, Auguft 24.

LA VENGEANCE, 52 : Taken by La Seine, 42, D. Milne, in the 'Mona Paffage, Weft Indies, Auguft 25, after a brilliant difplay of heroic ability for one hour and a half; in which La Seine had 13 killed, including 1 officer, and 28 wounded.

LA CAPRICIEUSE, (laden with arms,) 6 : Taken by the Termagant, (floop,) 18, W. Skipfey, 30 leagues weftward of Corfica, September 1.

L'ATENIENE, *(Maltefe,)*   64 : ⎫ Taken in the harbour of La Valette,
LE DEGO, *(Ditto,)*   64 : ⎬ Malta, (when that place furrendered,
LA CARTAGENOISE, *(Ditto,)* (frig.) ⎭ after blockade, to the Britifh forces,) September 4.   In addition to which were found there 2 merchant-fhips, (wanting repair,) 1 brig fit for fea, 1 xebec, fome gun-boats, &c.   The blockading force was commanded by Captain G. Martin, of the Northumberland, 74.

A SLOOP, (name unknown,) 8 : Taken by the Gipfy, (tender,) Lieut. Boger, near Guadaloupe, October 8.

LA VENUS, 32 : Taken by the Indefatigable, 44, Hon. H. Curzon, in company with the Fifgard, 44, T. B. Martin, Lifbon ftation, October 22.

A SHIP CORVETTE (name unknown) : Driven on fhore and burnt by the boats of Sir R. J. Strachan's fquadron, under the batteries of the Morbihan, November 17.

DUTCH

DUTCH NATIONAL SHIPS
LOST, TAKEN, or DESTROYED.

THE firſt Order of the Britiſh Government, for the Seizure and Detention of Dutch ſhips, proviſionally, was dated February 9, 1795; and His Majeſty's Order of Council, for making General Repriſals, was dated September 15 following.

1795.

*WILLEMSTADT, (now ⎫ Taken by the ſquadron under Vice-Admiral the Hon.
Princeſs,) 26 : ⎬ Sir G. K. Elphinſtone, K. B. in Simon's Bay, Cape of
STAR, (armed brig,) 14 : ⎭ Good Hope, Auguſt 18.

DE BRAK, (cutter,) 14 : Detained by the Fortune, 16, F. Woolridge, at Falmouth, Auguſt 20. Afterwards in the Britiſh ſervice, and loſt May 23, 1798. — *See Britiſh ſhips loſt, &c.*

*ALLIANCE, (now 20,) 36 : Taken by the Stag, 32, J. S. Yorke; in company with the Réunion, 36, J. Alms; Iſis, 50, R. Watſon; and Veſtal, 28, C. White; off the coaſt of Norway, Auguſt 22.

*COMET, (now *Penguin*,) 18 : Taken by the Unicorn, 32, T. Williams, on the Iriſh ſtation, Auguſt 28.

*OVERYSSEL, 64 : Taken poſſeſſion of at Cork, by the Polyphemus, 64, G. Lumſdaine, October 22.

MARIA LOUISA, (packet,) 14 : Taken by the Rattleſnake, 16, E. Ramage, off the Cape of Good Hope, October.

1796.

1796.

*ZEPHYR, (now *Evrus,)* 32 : Taken poffeffion of by the Andromeda, 32, W. Taylor ; Ranger, 16, J. Hardy ; and Kite, 18, M. Malbon; in the Frith of Forth, March.

*ZEELAND,   64 :⎫
*BRAKEL,   54 :⎬ Taken poffeffion of, as prizes, at Plymouth, by Vice-Admiral
*THOOLEN,   36 :⎬ Richard Onflow, and the fhips of war at that port,
*MIERMIN, (brig,) 16 :⎬ March 4.
*PYL, (brig,)   16 :⎭

THETIS,   24 :⎫Taken at the furrender of Demerary, April 23   *See colonies and*
ZEE MEEUV, 12 :⎬ *fettlements taken.* — The Thetis was afterwards funk at Demerary, and the Zee Meeuv loft.

*ARGO, (now *Janus,* 32,) 36 : Taken by the Phœnix, 36, L. W. Halfted, detached from the fleet of Admiral Duncan, in the North Sea. May 12.

ECHO, (brig,)   18 :⎫Run on-fhore by the Pegafus, 28, R. Donelly, detached from
DE GIER, (brig,) 14 :⎬ the fleet of Admiral Duncan, on the coaft of Friezeland, May 12.

MERCURY, (brig.) 10 : Taken by the Sylph, 16, J. C. White, (in fight of the fleet under Admiral Duncan,) off the Texel, May 12.   Afterwards in the Britifh fervice, named the *Hermes,* and loft, January, 1797.   *See Britifh fhips loft, &c.*

*JASON, (now *Profelyte,)* 32 : Brought into Greenock by her own crew, who mutinied, and taken poffeffion of by the Penguin, 18, J. K. Pulling, June 8.

*DORTRECHT,   64 :⎫Surrendered by Rear-Admiral Engelbertus Lucas, on capitula-
*REVOLUTIE,   ⎬ tion to, and taken poffeffion of by, the fquadron under Vice-
(now *P. Frederic,)* 64 :⎬ Admiral the Hon. Sir G. K. Elphinftone, K. B. in Sal-
*VAN TROMP,   54 :⎬ danha-Bay, near the Cape of Good Hope, without firing a
*CASTOR, (now   ⎬ gun, Auguft 17.   The Britifh fquadron confifted of the
Saldanha, 38,)   44 :⎬ Monarch, 74, Vice-Admiral the Hon. Sir G. K. Elphinftone,
*BRAAVE,   40 :⎬ Captain John Elphinftone ; Tremendous, 74, Rear-Admiral
*BELLONA, (now   ⎬ T. Pringle, Captain John Aylmer ; America, 64, Commo-
Vindictive,)   28 :⎬ dore J. Blanket ; Stately, 64, B. Douglas ; Ruby, 64, J.
*SIRENE, (now   ⎬ Waller ; Sceptre, 64, W. Effington ; Trident, 64, E. O.
Laurel,)   26 :⎬ Ofborn ; Jupiter, 50, G. Lofack ; Crefcent, 36, E. Buller ;
HAVICK,   18 :⎬ Sphinx, 24, A. Todd ; Mofelle, 16, Charles Brifbane ;
MARIA (ftore-fhip) :⎭ Rattlefnake, 16, E Ramage ; Echo, 16, John Turner ; and Hope, (floop,) J. Alexander.

BATAVE, 12 : Taken by the Roebuck, 44, A. S. Burrows, off Barbadoes, July 6.

*HAERLEM, (brig,) (now *Amboyna,)* 10 : Taken by the fquadron under Rear-Admiral P. Rainier, in the Eaft Indies.

D   1797.

1797

*VREYHEID, *(Liberty,)*	74:	Taken by the fleet under Admiral Adam Duncan,
Admiral de Winter:		off Camperdown, on the coaft of Holland,
*JUPITER, (now *Camperdown,)*	74:	October 11.
Vice-Admiral Reynties:		At 9 in the morning of that triumphant day,
*HAERLEM,	68:	a fquadron, acting under the orders of that ex-
*ADMIRAL DEVRIES,	68:	cellent officer Captain Henry Trollope, being
*GELYKHEID, *(Equality,)*	68:	feen with fignals flying for an enemy to leeward,
*WASSENAER,	64:	the fleet immediately bore up, and the Admiral,
*HERCULES, (now *Delft,)*	64:	having made fignal for a general chafe, foon ob-
DELFT,	56:	tained fight of them, forming, in a line, on the
*ALKMAAR.	56:	larboard tack The wind was at N.W. Shortly
MUNNIKKENDAM,	44:	after, the land, between Camperdown and
AMBUSCADE,	32:	Egmont, was feen about nine miles to leeward

of the enemy. The admiral's fignal was then made to bear up, to break their line, and engage
to leeward, each fhip her opponent. This was fkilfully effected, and thus the Britifh got between the enemy and the land, to which they were faft approaching.

Vice-Admiral Onflow, in the Monarch, bore down on the enemy's rear in the moft gallant
manner, his divifion following his example ; and the action commenced about 40 minutes paft
noon. The Venerable, Admiral Duncan's flag-fhip, foon paffed through the Dutch line, and
began a clofe action, with her divifion on the van of the enemy, which lafted near 2 hours and
a half, when all the mafts of the Vreyheid, Admiral de Winter's flag-fhip, went by the
board : but fhe was ftill defended in a moft heroic manner, until, being overpreffed by
numbers, her colours were ftruck. The vice-admiral's flag-fhip, the Jupiter, was alfo difmafted, and ftruck to Vice-Admiral Onflow ; and, at this time, many more had ftruck.
The fleet was now in 9 fathoms water, and not more than 5 miles from the coaft, upon which
the wind had conftantly blown ; and the fhips were, by that circumftance, much difperfed.
Thofe of the enemy which we have named were taken poffeffion of ; but the reft, taking
advantage of the night, and being fo near their own coaft, fucceeded in making their efcape
into the Texel. The fhips which efcaped were, — the States-General, 74, *Rear-Admiral
Story* ; Brutus, 74; *Cerberus, 68 ; *Leyden, 68 ; *Befchermer, 54 ; *Batavier, 54 ;
*Mars, 44 ; *Heldin, 32 ; *Minerva, 24; *Waakfaamheid, 26 ; Daphne, (brig,) 18 ;
Atalanta, 18 ; Ajax, 18 ; *Galathee, 16 ; and Haafje, 6. — Thofe to which this mark * is
affixed have been fince taken, as hereafter mentioned.

The names of the fhips which compofed the Britifh fleet, with the number of killed and
wounded in each refpectively, are as follows ; viz. Ruffel, 74, *H. Trollope, none k. 24 w.
— Director, 64, *W. Bligh, none k. 7 w. — Montague, 74, *J. Knight, 3 k. 5 w. —
Veteran, 64, *G. Gregory, 4 k. 21 w. — Monarch, 74, *Vice-Admiral R. Onflow, *Capt.
E. O'Bryen, 36 k. 100 w. — Powerful, 74, *W. O'Bryen Drury, 10 k. 78 w. — Monmouth,
64, *J. Walker, 5 k. 22 w. — Agincourt, 64, J. Williamfon, none k. or w. — Triumph,
74, *W. H. Effington, 29 k. 55 w. — Venerable 74, *Admiral A. Duncan, *Capt. W. G.
Fairfax,

Fairfax, 15 k. 62 w. — Ardent, 64, R. R. Burgefs, 41 k. 107 w. — Bedford, 74, *Sir T. Byard, 30 k. 41 w. — Lancafter, 64, *J. Wells, 3 k. 18 w. — Belliqueux, 64, *J. Inglis, 25 k 78 w. — Adamant, 50, * W. Hotham, none k. or w. — Ifis, 50, *W. Mitchell, 2 k. 21 w. — Thefe fhips formed the Brjtifh line ; to which may be added the following frigates, &c. which acted as repeaters of fignals, viz. the Beaulieu, 40, F. Fayerman ; Circe, 28, P. Halkett ; Martin, (floop,) 16, Hon. C. Paget ; Rofe, (hired cutter,) 10, Lieut. Jofeph Brodie ; King George, (hired cutter,) 12, Lieut. James Rains ; Active, (hired cutter,) 12, Lieut. J. Hamilton ; Diligent, (hired cutter,) 6, Lieut. T. Dawfon ; and Speculator, (hired lugger,) 8, Lieut. H. Hales. — Hence it appears that the total of the Britifh fleet was 24 fhips with 1198 guns, which had, in all, 203 killed and 539 wounded ; and that the total of the Dutch fleet was 26 fhips with 1255 guns ; of their lofs we poffefs no accurate account, but it was admitted that, in the two fhips only which bore the Admirals' flags, no lefs than 500 men were killed and wounded.

It is painful to ftate, that the brave Captain R. R. Burgefs, who brought the Ardent into action in the moft gallant and mafterly manner, was unfortunately killed foon after the engagement commenced.

For their meritorious conduct in this engagement, Admiral Duncan, his officers, and feamen, received the thanks of both Houfes of Parliament. The admiral was rewarded by his Majefty with the dignity of a vifcount of Great Britain, and a penfion of £3000 per annum for his public fervices. Vice-Admiral Onflow was created a baronet. The king was alfo pleafed to honor Captains H. Trollope and W. G. Fairfax with the order of knights-bannerets. Medals were likewife prefented to the flag-officers and captains of the line-of-battle fhips, as to thofe who particularly diftinguifhed themfelves in the engagement with Earl Howe, on the 1ft of June, 1794.—The names of the officers to whom medals were prefented are diftinguifhed above by this mark *.

The Delft unfortunately funk foon after the engagement, and fome of the people were loft. The Munnikkendam was alfo loft before fhe could be brought home ; the Ambufcade was likewife driven by rough weather on the coaft of Holland, and retaken ; but fhe has again been captured as ftated hereafter.

YONGE FRANK, (floop,)	10 :	Taken at Ternate ;
YONGE LANSIN, (floop,)	10 :	
WALKER, (floop,)	10 :	Taken off Celebes ;
LIMBI, (ketch,)	6 :	Taken at Gonontala, Ifland of Celebes ;
RESOURCE, (brig,)	6 :	Taken at Copang, in Timor ;

With feveral fmaller veffels ; by the Refiftance, 44, E. Pakenham, Eaft Indies.

1798.

DE COURIER, (pierced for 12,) 6 : Taken by the Scorpion, 16, J. T. Rodd, off Flamborough-Head, April 26.

*WAAKZAAMHEID,   26 : } Taken, with 6000 ſtand of arms and 540 men, by the
*FURIE, (now *Wilhelmina,)* 36 : }   Sirius, 36, R. King, in the North Sea; the former
in the morning, and the latter in the evening, of October 24.   Theſe ſhips, which ſailed together from the Texel on the night preceding their capture, had been waiting for an opportu-
nity of ſailing from July 21, and were little more than 2 miles aſunder when the Waakzaamheid was attacked the next morning by the captor.

1799.

CRASH, (G. V. *armed with carronades,)* 12 : Captured from the Britiſh, Auguſt 26, 1798.
Cut out and retaken, after an obſtinate reſiſtance, by the boats of the Pylades, (ſloop,) 18,
A. Mackenzie ; L'Eſpiegle, (brig.) 16, J. Boorder ; and Courier, (cutter,) 12, Lieut. T.
Scarle ; from Shiermannikoog, on the coaſt of Holland, Auguſt 11. At the ſame time, a
ſchooner of 70 men was burnt, and a row-boat of 30 men taken.
    UNDAUNTED, (G. B.) 2 : Taken by the boats of the Pylades, (ſloop,) 18, and others,
under the direction of Lieuts. Campbell and Humphries, within the Iſland of Shiermannikoog,
coaſt of Holland, Auguſt 13.
    VENGEANCE, (G. V.) 6 : Burnt to prevent being taken by ditto, Auguſt 14.
    *CAMPHAAN, (brig,) 16 : Taken, at the capitulation of Surinam, by the ſquadron un-
der Vice-Admiral Lord Hugh Seymour, Auguſt 20.

VERWACHTEN,	66 :	
BROEDERSCHAP,	54 :	
*HECTOR, (now *Pandour,)*	44 :	Taken poſſeſſion of, under the orders of Adm. Ld-
DUIFZE,	44 :	Viſc. Duncan, by the ſquadron of Vice-Adm. A.
EXPEDITIE,	44 :	Mitchell, conſiſting of the ſhips hereafter-men-
BELLE ANTOINETTE,	44 :	tioned, in the New Deep, in the Texel, Auguſt
CONSTITUTIE,	44 :	28, being the day on which the Britiſh troops
UNIE,	44 :	took poſſeſſion of the Helder-Point. Beſides which
*HELDIN,	32 :	were taken the Driegherlahn, Howda, and Vree-
*MINERVA, (now *Braak,)*	24 :	deluit, Indiamen, and a ſheer-hulk.
*VENUS, (now *L'Amaranthe,)*	24 :	
ALARM,	24 :	
*WASHINGTON, *Rear-Adm. Story,*	74 :	Surrendered to Vice-Admiral Mitchell's ſquadron,
(now *Prince of Orange,)*		within the Texel, Auguſt 30, without firing a
*GUELDERLAND,	68 :	gun. The Britiſh ſquadron conſiſted of the
*ADMIRAL DE RUYTER,	68 :	Glatton, 54, C. Cobb ; Romney, 50, J. Law-
UTRECHT,	68 :	ford ; Iſis, 50, Vice-Adm. Mitchell and Capt.
*CERBERUS, (now *Texel,)*	68 :	J. Oughton ; Veteran, 64, A. C. Dickſon ; Ar-
*LEYDEN,	68 :	dent, 64, T. Bertie ; Belliqueux, 64, R. Bul-
*BESCHERMER,	54 :	teel ; Monmouth, 64, G. Hart ; Overyſſel, 64,
*BATAVIER,	54 :	J. Bazely ; Miſtiloff, 60, *(Ruſſian,)* A. Mol-

*AM-

*AMPHITRITE,   44 :⎫   ler; Melpomene, 44, Sir C. Hamilton ; Latona,
*MARS, (now *Vlieter*,) 44 :⎬   38, F. Sotheron ; Shannon, 32, C D. Pater ; Juno,
*AMBUSCADE,   32 :⎭   32, G. Dundas ; and Lutine, 32, L. Skynner.
*GALATHEE,   16 :   The Ratvifan, Ruffian fhip, and America, 64, J.
Smith, grounded in going in ; and the fquadron were thus deprived of their affiftance.

The British fquadron, having gotten under-way in the morning, formed a line of battle, with a view of engaging the enemy in cafe of refiftance ; thus they paffed the Helder-Point and Mars-Diep, continuing their courfe along the Texel, into the channel that leads to the Vlieter; the Dutch fquadron then lying there at anchor, in a line, at the red buoy.   They then proceeded and anchored in a line at a fhort diftance from the Dutch fquadron, and, thus judicioufly difpofed, the Dutch admiral being fummoned to furrender, in lefs than an hour capitulated as aforefaid.

Thus did a Britifh fquadron, under an officer, who evinced, throughout this important enterprize, great boldnefs and judgement, by one grand and decifive ftroke, annihilate, with a very trivial exception, the fole remains of the NAVY of BATAVIA.

As a token of his royal approbation of the fervices of Vice-Adm. Mitchell, his Majefty was pleafed, fhortly after, to inveft him with the Order of the Bath.

DE VALK, 20 : Taken poffeffion of by Vice-Adm,' Mitchell, in the Zuyder-Zee, but loft on the Ifland of Ameland, Nov. 10, and only 29 perfons faved.

HERTOG VAN BRUNSWICK, *(Duke of Brunfwick,)* 50 : Taken by the Arrogant, 74, E. O. Ofborn, and Orpheus, 32, W. Hills, in the Straits of Sunda.

DE DRAAK,   24 :⎫ Taken by the Arrow, 30, N. Portlock, and Woolverine, (G. V.)
DE GIER, (brig,) 14 :⎭   12, W. Bolton, in the Vlie, near the Texel, Sept. 12. — De
                    Draak was afterwards deftroyed as unferviceable.

*DOLFYN, (now *Dolphin,)* 24 : Surrendered to the Arrow, 30, N. Portlock, and Woolverine, (G. V.) 12, at the Vlie-Ifland, September 15.

LYNX, (floop,)   12 :⎫ Taken, in the River Ems, by a *coup de main,* by the boats
PERSEUS, (fchooner,) 8 :⎭   of the Circe, 28, R. Winthrop, and Hawke, (cutter,)
12, Lieut. Matthew Buckle, under the direction of Lieuts. Maughan and Pawle, in the night of October 9.

FOUR GUN-BOATS, *each of four guns :* Cut out and taken from the Pampus, coaft of Holland, by the boats of the Dart, 30, P. Campbell, and of the gun-veffels, Hafty, Defender, Cracker, and Ifis, (fchoot,) October.

1800.

SPANISH

SPANISH NATIONAL SHIPS

LOST, TAKEN, or DESTROYED

WAR was proclaimed against Great Britain, at Madrid, October 8, 1796; and His Majesty's Order of Council, for general Reprisals, was issued on the 9th of the following Month.

1796.

LA PRINCESA, 16 : Detained by the Sea-Horse, 38, G. Oakes, off Corunna, Sept. 16.

EL MAHONESA, 34 : Taken, after a warm and spirited action of one hour and 40 minutes, by the Terpsichore, 32; R. Bowen, near Cape de Gatt, in the Mediterranean, October 13.

EL SAN PIO, (corveta,) 18 : Taken by the Regulus, 44, W. Carthew, on the Atlantic, November 2.

*EL GALGO, (corveta,) 18 : Taken, with 80,355 dollars, by the Alarm, 32, E. Fellowes, off Grenada, November 23.

*EL CORSO, (brig,) 18 : Taken by the Southampton, 32, J. Macnamara, near Cape Del Melle, in the Mediterranean, December 2.

LA SABINA, 40 : Taken by La Minerve, 42, C. Ogle, in the Mediterranean, December 20; but retaken the next day.

1797.

1797.

*SALVADOR DEL MUNDO, 112 :⎫ Taken by the fquadron under Admiral Sir John
*SAN JOSEF,   112 :⎬ Jervis, K. B. off Cape St. Vincent, February
*SAN NICOLAS,   80 :⎭ 14.
*SAN YSIDRO,   74 :⎭   The Spanifh fleet, from which thefe fhips
were cut off and captured, confifted of one fhip, El Santiffima Trinidada, of 136 guns ; 6 of
112 ; 2 of 84 ; 18 of 74; 12 frigates of 34 ; and one brig of 12 guns. Total, 27 large
fhips of the line, carrying 2308 guns, and 13 frigates, &c.—The Britifh fquadron confifted of
the Victory, 100, Adm. Sir J. Jervis, K. B. 1ft Captain, R. Calder ; 2d Captain, G. Grey ;
Britannia, 100, Vice-Adm. C. Thompfon, Capt. T. Foley , Barfleur, 98, Vice-Adm. Hon.
W. Waldegrave, Capt. J. R. Dacres · Prince George, 98, Rear-Adm. W. Parker, Capt. J.
Irwin ; Blenheim, 90, T. L. Frederick ; Namur, 90, J. H. Whitfhed ; Captain, 74, Com.
H. Nelfon, Capt. R. W. Miller ; Irrefiftible, 74, G. Martin ; Egmont, 74, J. Sutton ; Cul-
loden, 74, T. Trowbridge ; Orion, 74, Sir J Saumarez ; Coloffus, 74, G. Murray ; Excel-
lent, 74, C. Collingwood ; Goliath, 74, Sir C. H. Knowles, bart. ; and Diadem, 64, G. H.
Towry ; with the following frigates, &c. Lively, 32, Lord Vifcount Garlies ; La Minerve,
40, G. Cockburn ; Niger, 32, E·J. Foote ; Southampton, 32, J. Macnamara ; La Bonne Citoyenne, (floop,) 18, C. Lindfay ; Raven, (brig,) 18, W. Prowfe ; and Fox, (cutter,) 12,
Lieut. Gibfon. Total, 15 fhips of the line, carrying 1232 guns, and 7 frigates, &c.—Dif-
ference of guns, in favour of the Spanifh fleet, 1312 !

Previous notice of the fituation of the Spanifh fleet having been communicated to Adm. Sir
John Jervis, at the dawn of day of February 14, the Britifh being on the ftarboard-tack, with
Cape St. Vincent bearing E. by N. 8 leagues, a number of the Spanifh fhips were feen by the
Culloden and advanced frigates, extending from S. W. to S. At a quarter paft 8, the fquadron was ordered, by fignal, to form in clofe order, and, in a few minutes afterwards, to prepare for battle. The wind was at W. by S. and the weather extremely hazy. At half paft
ten, the enemy's fleet became vifible to all the fquadron, and appeared in two divifions, in no
regular order, the fhips firft difcovered and fubfequently captured being feparated from and to
leeward of the main body of the fleet.

The Britifh line, confifting only of the 15 fhips above-mentioned, was formed in the moft
compact order of failing in two columns ; and, by carrying a prefs of fail, got in between the
two divifions of the enemy's fleet before they had time to connect and form a regular order
of battle ; paffing through them, in a line formed with the utmoft celerity, they tacked, and
thereby feparated one-third from the main body. At about half paft 11, the fignal was made
to engage, and it was at this time that the van, led by the Culloden, Capt. Trowbridge, had
approached the enemy.

To defcribe diftinctly the various evolutions of the fhips, to expatiate on the conduct of
the heroes which commanded them, and to detail the various and innumerable inftances of
individual bravery difplayed in this engagement, would far, very far, exceed the limits of this
little work. It muft here fuffice, that, after a very long and arduous conteft, in which the tranf-
                                                                                      cendent

cendent fkill, activity, and bravery, of the feamen on one fide were as confpicuous as the vaft fuperiority of force in fhips on the other, the Salvador del Mundo, the rearmoft fhip of the enemy, ftruck to the admiral's fhip, and, at the fame time, the San Yfidro furrendered. The San Nicolas was boarded, in the boldeft manner, by a party from Commodore Nelfon's fhip, the Captain, headed by Lieutenant Berry, and joined by the commodore himfelf, whofe eager-nefs and intrepidity no danger could reprefs, and the fhip was quickly carried by the affail-ams. The Britifh were here annoyed by the mufquetry of the San Jofef, which was directly amidfhips on the weather-beam of the San Nicolas. The commodore, confiding in the bravery of his feamen, romantic as it may appear, refolved to advance into that fhip, and undauntedly headed his boarders in this frefh attack, which was equally crowned with fuccefs.

Night ended the conteft; and the clofe of day undoubtedly faved the Spanifh Admiral's fhip, which was a perfect wreck when the action ceafed, from falling into the hands of the victors.

Much of the glory of the day appears to be owing to the very great exertions of the fhips on the larboard tack: thofe which fuffered moft in the action were the Captain, Blenheim, Cul-loden, Excellent, and Irrefiftible. The Britifh had in all 73 killed and 223 wounded. The enemy had, in the 4 fhips taken, 261 killed and 342 wounded.

Admiral Jervis, his officers, and feamen, were honoured with the thanks of both Houfes of Parliament. Gold medals, &c. were fent out, by order of the King, and prefented to all the flag-officers and captains of fhips of the line, as to thofe who particularly fignalized them-felves with Earl Howe, on the 1ft of June, 1794. His Majefty was alfo pleafed to confer on the Admiral the dignity of an earl of the kingdom of Great Britain, and a penfion of £3000 per annum for his meritorious fervices. Vice-Admiral Thompfon and Rear-Admiral Parker were created baronets; Commodore Nelfon was invefted with the order of the Bath; and Captain R. Calder (now a baronet) was honoured with knighthood.

SAN VINCENTE, 84:⎫ Burnt, to prevent being taken, by the fleet under Rear-Ad-
GALI ARDO, 74:⎬ miral H. Harvey, in Shaggaramus-Bay, Ifland of Trinidad,
ARROGANTE, 74:⎪ Weft Indies, February 17.
SAN CECILIA, 36:⎭

SAN DAMASO, 74: Taken by the fleet under Rear-Admiral H. Harvey, in Shaggara-mus-Bay, Ifland of Trinidad, February 17.

LOS MAGELLANES, 4: Taken by the Dover, (A. T.) 44, Lieut. H. Kent, off the coaft of Portugal, March 12.

LA ELENA, 36: Deftroyed by the Irrefiftible, 74, G. Martin, in Conil-Bay, near Cadiz, April 26.

LA NIMFA, 36: Taken by the Irrefiftible, 74, G. Martin, Lifbon ftation. Afterwards in the Britifh fervice, named Hamadryad, and loft in 1798. *See Britifh fhips loft, &c.*

LA NUESTRA SENORA DE LA PIEDAD, 16 (fuppofed a privateer): Taken by the Viper, 12, Lieut. J. Pengelley, near Gibraltar, April 13.

LA NUESTRA SENORA DEL ROSARIO, 20: Taken by the Romulus, 36, G. Hope; and Mahonefa, 34, ———; off Cadiz, May 24. Afterwards in the Britifh fervice, called Rofario, and burnt in Dunkirk-Roads, July 7. — *See Britifh fhips loft, &c.*

SAN

SAN FRANCISCO, 14: Taken by the Santa Margarita, 36, G. Parker, off the coaft of Ireland, June 21.

EL BOLÁDER, 16: Taken by the Majeftic, 74, G. B. Weftcott, Lifbon ftation, November 14.

1798.

SAN ANTONIA, (packet,) 6: Taken by the Endymion, 44, Sir T. Williams, off the coaft of Ireland, May.

EL RECEVISO, (brig,) 6: Taken by the Aurora, 28, H. Digby, Lifbon ftation, May 8.

*SANTA DOROTHEA, 42: Taken by the Lion, 64, M. Dixon, in the Mediterranean, Carthagena bearing nearly W. by N. 29 leagues diftant.   The Dorothea, accompanied by the Pomone, 44 ; Cafilda, 42 ; and Proferpine, 42 ; who had failed on a cruize from Carthagena on the 8th of July ; were brought to clofe action by the Lion on the 15th, at about 11 A. M. which lafted, with great warmth, till 10 minutes paft 1, when they were defeated, leaving the Dorothea, in great diftrefs, to the mercy of the captor.   The manly and fpirited conduct of Captain Dixon in and fubfequent to the action reflects on him and his company great honour, and merits univerfal applaufe.

LA VELOSA ARRAGONESA, (armed en flute,) 30 : Taken by the Aurora, 28, H. Digby, off the Açores, or Weftern Iflands, September 16.

SAN LEON, (brig,) 16: Taken by the Santa Dorothea, 42, H. Downman; Strombolo, 8, J. Broughton; Perfeus, 10, James Ofwald; and Bull-Dog, 14, A. Drummond; Lifbon ftation, November 24.

FOURTEEN GUN-VESSELS : Taken at the capture of the Ifland of Minorca, Nov. 15.

PETERELL, (floop,) 16: Retaken by the Argo, 44, J. Bowen, in the Mediterranean, Nov. 13, having been captured, the preceding day, by the three Spanifh frigates which efcaped from the Lion, 64, on the 15th of July. — See Santa Dorothea above.

1799.

EL VALIANTA, (packet,) 12 : Taken by the Cormorant, 20, Lord M. R. Kerr, near Malaga, in the Mediterranean, January 2.

*SANTA TERESA, 42: Taken by the Argo, 44, J. Bowen, (the Leviathan, 74, in fight,) near Majorca, in the Mediterranean, February 6.

AFRICA, (xebec,) 14: Taken by L'Efpoir, 16, J. Sanders, after a fharp conteft of nearly two hours, in which the Britifh very gallantly boarded, Mediterranean, Feb. 22.

EL GUADALOUPE, 40 : Run on-fhore, near Cape Oropefa, Mediterranean, by the Centaur, 74, J. Markham ; and Cormorant, 20, Lord M. R. Kerr; and totally loft, March 16.

EL GOLANDRINA, (packet,) 20 : Taken by the Mermaid, 32, J. Newman, and Sylph, 14, J. C. White, off Corunna, March 24.

URCA CARGADORA, 12: Burnt by La Prompte, 20, T. Dundas, Weft Indies, March.

*EL

*EL VINCELO, (brig) 18 : Taken by the Cormorant, 20, Lord M. R. Kerr, Mediterranean, March 19.

ST. ANTONIO, (brig,) 14 : Taken by the Terpsichore, 32, W. H Gage, Mediterranean, June 23.

EL PAXARO, (packet,) *(pierced for* 16,) 4. Taken by the Alarm, 32, Robert Rolles, in the Gulf of Florida, May.

LA FELIZ, (schooner) 14: Taken by the Alarm, 32, Robert Rolles, (Hannibal, 74, and Thunderer, 74, in fight,) West Indies, July.

SANTA DORVAL, (packet,) 4 : Taken by the York, 64, J. Ferrier; in company with the Carnatic, 74; Thunderer, 74; Alarm, 32 ; and Volage, 22 ; in the West Indies, July.

*INFANTA AMELIA, (now *Porpoise,)* (packet,) 12 : Taken by the Argo, 44, J. Bowen, off the coast of Portugal, August 6.

A GUN-BOAT, *(brass* 18-*pounders,)* 2 : ⎱ Taken by the Mayflower Privateer, of Guern-
A PACKET,   8 : ⎰ sey, J. Le Barr, Mediterranean, September.

EL THETIS, 40 : Taken, after a well-directed fire of 2 broadsides, and a running fight of half an hour, by the Ethalion, 38, J. Young; in company, with the Naiad, 38, W. Pierrepont ; Alcmene, 32, H. Digby ; and Triton, 32, J. Gore ; near Ferrol, October 17.

SANTA BRIGIDA, 40 : Taken by the Naiad, 38, W. Pierrepont ; Alcmene, 32, H. Digby ; and Triton, 32, J. Gore; a little to the southward of Cape Finisterre, October 18.

⁎ The Thetis and Santa Brigida had left Vera Cruz, in Mexico, on the 21st of August. The former with 1,411,526 dollars, and a valuable cargo of cocoa ; and the latter with 1,400,000 dollars, and a cargo of equal estimation. They were first fallen in with by the Naiad, at 8 in the evening of the 16th of October, in latitude 44° 1′ N. and longitude 12° 35′ W. who immediately gave chase. Before midnight she was joined by the Ethalion ; and, at break of day, the next morning, by the Alcmene ; when the Triton, which afterwards joined, was descried far astern. The Ethalion, by signal, stood for, engaged, and captured, the headmost ship, as described above ; but the Santa Brigida, by her superior sailing, made off, and rounded Cape Finisterre, with an intention to escape into Port de Vidre or Muros ; and it was here, at 8 in evening of the 18th, amidst the rocks of Commarurto, near the entrance of Muros, that her colours were struck.

*HERMIONE, (now *Retribution,* 32,) 44 : Run away with by the crew in 1797. — *See British ships lost, &c.* — Cut out of Porto Cavallo, in the West Indies, from under the batteries, on which were mounted 200 pieces of cannon, by the boats of the Surprise, 32, led on by her captain, Edward Hamilton, October 25.

For this daring, and almost unparalleled, enterprize, the boats were manned with 100 men, including officers : of which, according to Captain Hamilton's disposition for the attack, 50, with himself, should board, while the remainder, in the boats, cut the cables, and took the ship in tow: from this manœuvre he formed the idea that, while he was disputing for the possession of the ship, she was approaching the Surprise, which was lying close to the harbour, and, in case he was beaten out, the contest could be taken up on more favourable terms.

This

This plan was steadily executed. — At half past 12, in the morning of the 25th of October, (after having beat off the launch of the ship, which carried a 24-pounder and 20 men,) the 50 men with Captain Hamilton boarded; the forecastle was taken possession of without much resistance; the quarter-deck disputed for a quarter of an hour, where a dreadful carnage ensued; the main-deck held out much longer, and with equal slaughter; nor was it before both cables were cut, sail made on the ship, with the boats a-head to tow, that the main-deck was secured: the enemy at last retreated to between decks, and fired till their ammunition was expended; then, and not till then, did they cry for quarter. At two o'clock the Hermione was out of gun-shot of the fort, and completely secured. Previous to her re-capture she was nearly ready for sea, having been thoroughly repaired; she then mounted 44 guns, and had 392 persons on-board, of whom 119 were killed, and 97 wounded. Of the British, none were killed, and only 12 wounded, including the captain. — His Majesty was pleased, shortly after, to confer on Captain Hamilton the honour of knighthood, and to present him with a medal, similar to those given to the illustrious characters distinguished in the four grand engagements.

EL GALGO, (corveta,) 16: Taken by the Crescent, 36, W. G. Lobb, on her passage to the West Indies, November 15. Afterwards in the British service, and lost, 1800. — *See British ships lost, &c.*

1800.

DEL CARMEN, (xebec-corveta,) 16: Taken by the Penelope, 36, H. Blackwood, Mediterranean, January 26.

EL CURBO, (packet,) *(pierced for 16,)* 4: Taken by the Alarm, 32, R. Rolles, off Cape Catouche, in the West Indies, February.

*DEL CARMEN, 36 : ⎱ Each laden with 1500 quintals of quicksilver, &c. Taken by the
*FLORENTIA, 36 : ⎰ Leviathan, 74, Rear-Admiral J. T. Duckworth, Captain J. Carpenter, and Emerald, 36, T. M. Waller, near Cadiz, April 7.

CORTES, (packet,) *(pierced for 14,)* 4: Taken by the Flora, 36, R. G. Middleton, Lisbon station, June 22.

GIBRALTAR, (G. B.) 10 : ⎱ Taken by the Anson, 44, P. C. Durham, near Gibraltar,
SALVADOR, (G. B.) 10 : ⎰ June 29.

DEL CARMEN, (felucca,) . 2 : Destroyed by the Bonetta, 18,⎫
                                           H. Vanfittart, ⎪ Jamaica station,
A GUN-BOAT, (name unknown,) 2 : Taken by the Rattler, 16, ⎬ between May
                                           J. M. Spread, ⎪ and August.
A SHIP, (name unknown,) 18 : Taken by the Apollo, 36,⎭
                                           P. Halkett.

EL BELOZ, (brig-packet,) *(pierced for 16,)* 4: Taken by the Clyde, 38, C. Cunningham, Channel station, August 20.

EL VIVO, (brig,) 14: Taken by the Fisgard, 44, T. B. Martin, off the coast of Spain, September 30.

CONCEPTION,

CONCEPTION, alias   ⎧ Corvettes, which appear to have been intended for a secret
  Efmiralda,   22 : ⎬ expedition ; cut out of Barcelona-Road, Mediterranean, in
LA PAZ,   22 : ⎭ the boldeft ftyle, by the boats of the Minotaur, 74, T.
Louis; and Niger, 32, James Hillyar; headed by Captain Hillyar, Lieutenant Schomberg,
of the Minotaur, and other Lieutenants, after an action of one hour, under a heavy fire from
the fhips, four ftrong batteries, &c. and fhells from the fort of Mount Joni, in the night of
September 3.

SAN JOSEF, alias *L'Aglies*, (polacre,) 14 : Boarded, in the *ufual manner*, which language
is almoft inadequate to defcribe, and brought out, in oppofition to a warm refiftance made
with mufquetry and fabres, by the boats of the Phaeton, 38, J. N. Morris, directed by
Lieutenant F. Beaufort, near Malaga, in the night of October 25. Lieutenant Beaufort, and
three others, were feverely wounded. The Spaniards, befides fome which appear to have been
driven over-board, had 13 wounded.

BRITISH

BRITISH SHIPS of WAR

LOST, TAKEN, or DESTROYED,

FROM THE COMMENCEMENT OF HOSTILITIES

In FEBRUARY, 1793.

1793.

*HYÆNA, 24, William Hargood, B 1778 : Captured by La Concorde, 40, off Hifpaniola, May. Afterwards a privateer, and re-taken in 1797. — *See French privateers taken, &c.*

*THAMES, 32, J. Cotes, B. 1758 : Captured, in going to Gibraltar, by the Carmagnol, and two other frigates, October 24, after having been engaged, in the morning of that day, for upwards of 4 hours with a French frigate, which then made off. Retaken June 7, 1796.

PIGMY, (cutter,) 14, A. Pulliblank, P. 1782 : Loft in the Channel, December, with the crew.

VULCAN, (F. S.) 14, C. Hare, B. 1783 : Burnt at Toulon, December 18, in deftroying the French fhips. Crew faved. — *See French fhips loft, &c.*

AMPHITRITE, 24, A. Hunt, B. 1778 : Loft in the Mediterranean, by ftriking on a funken rock. Crew faved.

CONFLAGRATION, (F. S.) 14, J. Loring, B. 1783 : Burnt at Toulon, to prevent falling into the hands of the enemy, December 18.

ADVICE, (cutter,) 14, Lieut. E. Tyrrel : Loft in the Bay of Honduras. Crew faved.

E

1794.

LA MOSELLE, 20, H. A. Bennett, T. 1793: Retaken at Toulon, after the evacuation, January 7. Again taken by the British, May 23. — *See French ships lost, &c.*

CONVERT, (formerly *Inconstant,)* 36, J Lawford, T. 1793: Lost on the Grand Caymanes, West Indies, March 8. Crew saved.

SPITFIRE, (schooner,) 8, T. W. Rich, P. 1793: Overset off St. Domingo, February, and lost with all the crew.

ARDENT, 64, R. M. Sutton, B. 1782: Lost off Corsica. Supposed to be blown up by accident, with the crew.

*CASTOR, 32, T. Troubridge, B. 1785: Taken off Cape Clear, May 9; retaken May 29, 1794. — *See French ships lost, &c.*

ALERT, 18, C. Smyth, B. 1793: Taken by L'Unité, 40, off the coast of Ireland, May. Run on-shore, and lost, August 23, following. — *See French ships lost, &c.*

*L'ESPION, (sloop,) 18, W. H. Kittoe, P. 1794: Taken by three French frigates. Retaken March 2, 1795. — *See French ships lost, &c*

*SPEEDY, (sloop,) 14, G. Eyre, B. 1782: Taken off Nice, June. Retaken March, 1795. — *See French ships lost, &c.*

LA PROSELYTE, (floating battery,) 24, T. 1793: Sunk, off Bastia, by the fire of the French batteries, May.

ROSE, 28, M. Scott, B. 1783: Lost on Rocky-Point, Jamaica, June 28. Crew saved.

*RANGER, (now *La Venturier,)* (cutter,) 14, Lieutenant Cotgrave, P. 1787: Taken off Brest, June. Retaken. Again captured, — and finally retaken, November 6, 1797. — *See French ships lost, &c.*

HOUND, 16, R. Piercy, B. 1790: Taken by La Seine and Galatea, French frigates, coming from the West Indies, July 14.

SCOUT, 18, C. Robinson, B. 1778: Taken by two French frigates, off Cape Bona, August. (Since lost.)

L'IMPÉTUEUX, 78, T. 1794: Burnt, by accident in Portsmouth-harbour, August 29. Crew saved.

*ALEXANDER, 74, Rear-Admiral R. R. Bligh, B. 1778: Taken, after a truly honourable and gallant defence, by a French squadron of five 74 s and three frigates, off Scilly, Nov. 6. Retaken, by Admiral Lord Bridport, June 23, 1795 — *See French ships lost, &c.*

PLACENTIA, (sloop,) Lieutenant A. Sheppard, B. 1790: Lost at Newfoundland. Crew saved.

L ACTIF, (F.) 16, John Harvey, T. 1794: Foundered off Bermuda, November 26. Crew saved.

1795.

*DAPHNE, 20, W. E. Cracraft, B. 1776: Taken by two french men of war, February 12. Retaken December 28, 1797. — *See French ships lost, &c.*

BER-

SERWICK, 74, Adam Littlejohn, B. 1775 : Taken by the French fleet in the Mediterranean, March 7. Captain Littlejohn, in its defence, was unfortunately killed.

ILLUSTRIOUS, 74, T. L. Frederick, B. 1789 : Loft in a gale on the rocks near Avenza, Mediterranean, March 14. Crew faved.

BOYNE, 98, George Grey, B. 1790 : Burnt, by accident, at Spithead, May 1. Crew faved.

MUSQUITO, (G.V.) 5, Lieutenant M'Carthy, B. 1794 : Loft on the coaft of France, near Jerfey, and all the crew.

*NEMESIS, 28, S. H. Linzee, B. 1780 : Taken by three French frigates, in the port of Smyrna. Retaken March 9, 1796. — *See French fhips loft, &c.*

FLYING 'FISH, (fchooner,) Lieutenant Seton, B. 1795 : Taken by two French privateers, Windward-paffage, Weft Indies, June. Retaken May 5, 1796.

DIOMEDE, 44, Matthew Smith, B. 1782 : Struck on a funken rock and foundered off Trincomale, in the ifland of Ceylon, Auguft 2. Crew faved.

LE CENSEUR, 74, J Gore, T. 1795 : Retaken by a fquadron of French fhips, confifting of 6 of the line and 3 fr gates, (Cape St. Vincent 83 leagues diftant,) October 7. Le Cenfeur was in company with the Bedford, 74 ; Fortitude, 74 ; and Lutine, 32 ; having under their convoy a large fleet of merchant-fhips from Gibraltar, part of which were captured.

LA FLECHE, 14, C. Came, T. 1794 : Loft in St. Fiorenzo Bay, November 12. Crew faved.

SHARK, (D.H.) 4, Lieutenant Watfon, P. 1794 : Ran away with by the crew into La Hogue, Dec. 11.

AMETHYST, 36, F. T. Affleek, T. 1793 : Loft at Alderney, December 29. Crew faved.

1796.

SCOURGE, (floop,) 16, William Stap, B. 1779 : Loft off the coaft of Holland.

LEDA, 36, John Woodley, B. 1783 : Foundered near Madeira. The crew, except 7, loft, February 11.

CA IRA, 80, C. D. Pater, T. 1795 : Burnt, by accident, in St. Fiorenza Bay, April 11. Loft 4 men.

SALISBURY, 50, W. Mitchell, B. 1769 : Loft on the Ifle of Avache, St. Domingo, May 13. Crew faved.

ARAB, 18, S. Seymour, T. 1795 : Loft on the Penmarks, near Breft, June 10. Crew faved.

LA TROMPEUSE, (F.) 18, J. R. Watfon, T. 1794 : Loft on the Farmer-Rock, Kinfale. Crew faved.

ACTIVE, 32, E. L. Gower, B. 1780 : Loft in the river St. Laurence, July. Crew faved.

LA SIRENNE, 16, D. Guerin, T. 1794 : Loft in the Bay of Honduras, with the crew, Auguft.

CORMORANT, (floop,) 16, T. Gott, B. 1794: Blown up at Port-au-Prince, Weft Indies, October 14, and only 20 men faved.

AMPHION, 32, I. Pellew, B. 1780 : Blown up, by accident, in Hamoaze, Plymouth, and moft of the crew perifhed, September 22.

BERMUDA, (floop,) 18, T. Maxtone, B. 1795: Suppofed to be loft, with the crew, in the Gulph of Florida, September.

MALABAR, 54, T. Parr, P. 1795: Foundered in coming from the Weft Indies, Oct. 10. Crew faved.

LA POULETTE, 26, J Edwards, T. 1793 : Burnt at Ajacio, Oct. 20, being unferviceable.

LA BELETTE, 24, J. Temple, T. 1793 : Burnt at Ajacio, October 20, being unferviceable.

EXPERIMENT, (lugger,) 10, Lieutenant G. Hayes, B. 1793 : Taken by the Spaniards, in the Mediterranean, October 2.

LE VANNEAU, (F.) 6, Lieutenant J. Gourly, T. 1793 : Loft at Port Ferajo, Mediterranean, November. Crew faved.

HELENA, (floop,) 14, J. Symons, B. 1778 : Loft on the coaft of Holland, November 3. Crew loft.

BIRBICE, (fchooner,) J. Trefahar, P. 1793 : Driven on-fhore at Dominica, November. Crew faved.

LA REUNION, (F.) 36, H. W. Bayntun, T. 1793: Loft in the Swin. Crew faved, except 3, December 7.

UNDAUNTED, 40, Robert Winthrop, T. 1793 : Foundered on the Morant-Keys, Weft Indies. Crew faved, Auguft 27.

COURAGEUX, 74, B Hallowell, T. 1761 : Loft near the foot of Apes' Hill, Straits of Gibraltar, and only 124 of the crew faved, Dec. 18.

BOMBAY-CASTLE, 74, T. Sotheby, B, 1782 : Loft in the River Tagus, December. Crew faved.

NARCISSUS, 20, P. Frafer, B. 1781: Loft in the Weft Indies, October 3. Crew faved.

CURLEW, (F.) 18, V. Field, B. 1795 : Foundered in the North Sea, with the crew, December 31.

HUSSAR, 28, J. Colnett, B. 1784 : Loft on the coaft of France, Dec. 27. Crew faved.

1797.

LA VIPERE, 18, H. H. Parker, T. 1794: Loft off the Shannon, Jan. 2, with the crew.

AMAZON, 36, R. C. Reynolds, B. 1795: Loft near the Ifle of Bas. coaft of France, January 14. Crew faved by the French.

HERMES, 16, William Mulfo, T. 1796 : Loft at fea, in January, with all the crew.

BLOOM, (tender,) 14, Lieutenant H. Congalton, P. 1795 : ⎱ Taken off Holyhead, in the
BRIGHTON, (tender,) 14, P. 1795 : ⎰ Irifh Sea, Feb. 24.

ALBION, 60, H. Savage, B. 1763: Loft on the Middle-Sand, in the Swin, April 27. Crew faved.

TAR-

TARTAR, 28, Hon. C. Elphinftone, B. 1756 : Loft at St. Domingo, April.   Crew faved by the Sparrow, (cutter,) 12, J. C. Peers.

LACEDEMONIAN, 12, M. Wrench, P. 1796 : Taken in the Weft Indies, May.

*FORT ROYAL, (fchooner,) 10, Lieutenant Mann, P. 1796 : Taken and carried into Port-àu-Paix, Weft Indies, May.   Afterwards retaken ; and now named *Recovery*.

LA MIGNONNE, 32, P. Wodehoufe, T. 1794 : Burnt as unferviceable, at Ferrajo, Corfica, July 31.

ARTOIS, 38, Sir E. Nagle, B. 1794 : Loft on the coaft of France, July 31.   Crew faved.

FOX, (cutter,) 12, Lieutenant J. Gibfon : Deftroyed at Teneriffe, the commander killed, and only 16 of the crew faved.   July 24.

FORTUNE, (floop,) 16, V. Collard, B. 1778 : Loft near Oporto.

*HERMIONE, 32, H. Pigot, B. 1782 : Run away with by the crew in the Weft Indies, Sept. 22, who affaffinated the captain.   Retaken by the Surprife, 32, E. Hamilton, Oct. 25, 1799.   *See Spanifh fhips loft, &c.*   Now called the *Retribution*.

MARIE ANTOINETTE, (fchooner,) 10, Lieutenant J. M'Inerheny, T. 1793 : Run away with by the crew, in the Weft Indies, who murdered the captain.

LE TRIBUNE, 44, S. Barker, T. 1796 : Wrecked off Hallifax.   Officers and crew loft, except 7.   November.

PROVIDENCE, 16, W. R. Broughton, P. 1797 : Sailed on difcoveries, February, 1795.   Loft May 16, 1797.   Crew faved.

PANDOUR, 14, Lieutenant S. Mafon, T. 1795 : Loft in the North Sea. with the crew.

HOPE, (lugger,) 10 (hired) : Run down and foundered in the Channel, November.

RESOLUTION, (brig,) 14, Lieutenant William Huggett, P: 1779 : Loft on a cruife, with all the crew.

HUNTER, 16, Tudor Tucker, B. 1796 : Loft on Hog-Ifland, off Virginia, crew faved, except 5, December 27, 1797.

GROWLER, (G.V.) 12, Lieutenant J. Hollingfworth, B. 1794 : Taken on Dungenefs by two French row-boats, December.

SWIFT, (floop,) 16, T. Hayward, B. 1793 : Loft in the China Seas with all the crew ; time unknown.

1798.

ROVER, 18, G. Irvine, B. 1796 : Loft in the Gulf of St. Lawrence.   Crew faved.

GEORGE, (floop,) Lieutenant Mackay : Taken by two Spanifh privateers, in the Weft. Indies, January 3.

RAVEN, (brig,) 18, J. W. T. Dixon, B. 1795 : Loft in the North Sea, February 4.   Crew faved.

HAMADRYAD, 36, T. Elphinftone, T. 1797 : Loft in the Bay of Algiers.   Crew faved.

PALLAS, 32, Hon. H. Curzon, B. 1794 : Loft on Mount-Batten Point, Plymouth-Sound, April 4.   Crew faved.

LIVELY, 32, J. N. Norris, B. 1794 : Loft on Rota-Point, near Cadiz.   Crew faved.

DE BRAK, 14, James Drew, T. 1795 : Upfet in the Delaware. Captain and 34 of the crew loft. May 23.

LA PIQUE, 36, D. Milne, T. 1795 : Run aground and bilged on the coaft of France, June 29. Crew faved.

L'ETRUSCO, 24, G. Reynolds, P. 1794 : Foundered in coming from the Weft Indies, Auguft 25. Crew faved.

RESISTANCE, 44, E. Pakenham, B. 1782 : Struck by lightning and blew up, in the Eaft Indies, with her brave and ingenious captain, Auguft. The crew, excepting 5, were loft.

*LEANDER, 50, T. B. Thompfon, B. 1780 : Taken in the Mediterranean, September 1, (on her return to England, having fuffered in the battle of the Nile,) by Le Généreux, 74, (which efcaped in that engagement,) after a moft fevere action of 6 hours. Retaken at Corfu, by the Ruffians and Turks, March 3, 1799, and reftored to Britain by the Emperor of Ruffia. The Généreux was captured February 18, 1800. — See French fhips loft, &c.

JASON, 38, C. Stirling, B. 1794 : Run aground near Breft, and loft, October 13. Crew faved, but made prifoners.

*CRASH, (G. V.) 12, Lieutenant B. M. Praed, B. 1797 : Taken on the coaft of Holland, Auguft 26. Retaken Auguft 11, 1799. — See Dutch fhips loft, &c.

GARLAND, 28, J. A. Wood, B. 1779 : Loft off the coaft of Madagafcar, July 26. Crew faved.

NEPTUNE, (lugger,) 6, R. Gormer (hired): Run down, off Beachey-Head, and foundered.

PRINCESS ROYAL, (cutter,) 8, R. Keys (hired) : Taken by a French privateer in the North Sea, July.

L'AIGLE, 38, C. Tyler, T. 1782 : Loft on the coaft of Barbary. Crew faved.

MARGARET, (tender,) Lieutenant J. Pollexfen, B. 1785 : Loft off the coaft of Ireland. with all the crew. November.

MEDUSA, 50, A. Becher, B. 1785 : Driven on-fhore and rendered unferviceable, Lifbon ftation, November 22.

KING's FISHER, (brig,) 18, F. L. Maitland, B. 1787 : Loft on the bar of Lifbon, December 3. Crew faved.

COLOSSUS, 74, G. Murray, B. 1794 : Loft off Scilly, December 10. Crew faved.

*PETERELL, (floop,) 16, C. Long, B. 1773 : Taken by three Spanifh frigates, off Majorca, Dec. 14, but retaken by the Argo, 44, J. Bowen, on the next day. — See Spanifh fhips loft, &c.

AMBUSCADE, 32, H. Jenkins, B. 1794 : Taken by the Bayonaife, 32, in the Bay of Bifcay, after a fevere engagement, December 14.

CAROLINE, (tender,) Lieutenant Whittle, H. 1798 : Loft in the Eaft Indies. Crew never heard of.

1799.

APOLLO, 38, P. Halkett, B. 1783 : Loft on the coaft of Holland, Jan. 7. Crew faved.

WEAZLE, (floop,) 12, Hon. H. Grey, B. 1777 : Loft in Barnftaple-Bay, with all the crew except the purfer, Mr. S. Haly, January 12.   PRO-

PROSERPINE, 28, James Wallis, B. 1784: Loft in the Elbe, February 1. Crew faved, except 15.

NAUTILUS, (floop,) 16, H. Gunter, B. 1784: Loft off Flamborough-Head, Feb. 2. Crew faved.

GRAMPUS, (S. S.) 54, G. Hall, B. 1795: Grounded and loft on Barking-Shelf, near Woolwich, in the River Thames, February. Crew faved.

CHARLOTTE, (fchooner,) 10, Lieutenant Thickneffe, P. 1798: Taken off Cape François. Retaken near Cape Tiberon, November 22, 1799. — *See French ships loft, &c.*

MUSQUITO, 16, Lieutenant White, P. 1794: Taken, by two Spanifh frigates, off Cuba.

BRAVE, (lugger,) 12, Lieutenant H. Guion (hired): Run down, off Beachy-Head, by a tranfport, April 22. Crew faved.

LES DEUX AMIS, (floop,) 14, S. Wilfon, T. 1796: Loft on the back of the Ifle of Wight, May 23. Crew faved.

WILLIAM PITT, (lugger,) 14, Lieutenant Hafwell (hired): Captured by Spanifh gun-boats in the Mediterranean, June 6.

PENELOPE, (cutter,) 18, Lieutenant D. Hamline (hired): Taken by the N. S. del Carmen, Spanifh frigate, in the Mediterranean, July 7.

CONTEST, (G. V.) 12, J. J. Short, B. 1794: Loft off the coaft of Holland. Crew faved.

TRINCOMALEE, (floop,) 16, J. Rowe, P. 1799: Blown up in an engagement with a French fhip, in the Straits of Babelmandel, October 12. All the crew perifhed as well as the French fhip.

BLANCHE, 32, J. Ayfcough, B. 1786: Loft in the Texel, September 28. Crew faved.

FOX, (fchooner,) 18, Lieutenant Woolridge: Loft in the Gulf of Mexico, Sept. 28. Crew faved.

LA LUTINE, 32, L. Skynner. T. 1793: Loft off the Vlie Ifland, coaft of Holland, Oct. 9. Crew loft, except 2.

IMPREGNABLE, 90, J. Faulkner, B. 1786: Loft between Langftone and Chichefter, October 19. Crew faved.

NASSAU, 64, G. Tripp, B. 1785: Loft on the coaft of Holland, October 14, with 42 of the crew.

L'ESPION, (formerly *L'Atalante,)* 38, J. Rofe, T. 1794: Loft on the Goodwin-Sands, November 16. Crew faved.

SCEPTRE, 64, V. Edwards, B. 1781: Loft in Table-Bay, Cape of Good Hope, Dec. 5, with 291 of the crew.

ETHALION, 38, J. C. Searle, B. 1797: Loft on the Penmarks, Dec. 25. Crew faved.

L'AMARANTHE, (floop,) 16, J. Blake, T. 1796: Loft on the coaft of Florida, 20 leagues to the fouthward of Cape Canaverel, and many of the crew perifhed on-fhore with hunger, September.

1800.

MASTIFF, (G. B.) 12, Lieutenant J. Watfon: Loft on Yarmouth-Sands, with 8 of the crew, January 5.   BRAZEN,

BRAZEN, (floop,) 18, J. Hanfon, B. 1799 : Loft near Brighton, Jan. 26.   Only 1 man faved.

WEYMOUTH, (A. T.) 26, A Crofton, P. 1796 : Loft on the bar of Lifbon, Jan. 21. Crew faved.

REPULSE, 64, J. Alms, B. 1780 : Loft on a funken rock, 25 leagues S. E. of Ufhant, March 10.   Crew (except 10) faved on the Glenan Iflands, but made prifoners.

DANAE, (formerly *La Vaillante,*) 20, Lord Proby, T. 1798 : Carried into Breft by mutiny of the crew, March 17.

QUEEN CHARLOTTE, 100, Vice-Admiral Lord Keith, Captain A. Todd, B. 1790 : Blown up, with the captain, in Leghorn-Roads, after having caught fire by accident, only 24 officers, and 144 feamen, efcaping, March 17.

RAILEUR, 20, J. Ravnor, (F. Pr. P.) :   ⎫ Parted in a gale in the Channel,
LA TROMPEUSE, 18. J. P. Robinfon, (F. Pr. P.) : ⎬ May 16 or 17, and not fince
LADY JANE, (cutter,) 8, W. Bryer (hired) :   ⎭ heard of.

WASP, (F. V.) 16, J. Edwards, P. 1782 :   ⎫ Burnt in Dunkirk-Roads, in attempting
FALCON, (F. V.) 14, H. S. Butt, B. 1782 : ⎬ to deftroy fome French frigates, July
COMET, 14, (Bb.) T. Leef, B. 1783 :   ⎬ 7.
ROSARIO, S. (F. S.) 14, J. Carthew, T. 1797 : ⎭

DROMEDARY, (S. S.) 24, B. W. Tayler, B. 1799 : Loft in the Bocca, near the Ifland of Trinidad, in the night of Auguft 10.   Crew faved.

STAG, 32, R. Winthrop, B. 1794 : Loft in Vigo-Bay, September 6.   Crew faved.

HOUND, (brig,) 18, W. J. Turquand, B; 1796 : Loft near Shetland, September 26. Crew loft.

CORMORANT, 20 : Hon. C. Boyle, T. 1796 : Loft on the coaft of Egypt.   Crew faved, but made prifoners by the French.

CHANCE, S. (floop,) G. S. Stovin, 16, (late *Galgo,*) T. 1799 : Upfet on her beam-ends, and foundered in the Weft Indies, October 9.   Only 2 officers and 23 men faved.

ROSE, (hired cutter,) 10, Lieutenant Smith : Captured, by two Dutch gun-veffels, in the river Ems, October 13.

MARLBOROUGH, 74, T. Sotheby, B. 1767 : Loft on a funken rock, near Belle Ifle, November 4.   Crew faved.

HAVICK, (floop,) 18, P. Bartholmew, T. 1796 : ⎱ Loft in St. Aubin's Bay, Jerfey,
PELICAN, (brig,) 18, J. Thicknefle, B 1795 :   ⎰ November 9.   Crews faved.

ACTIVE, (cutter,) 12, Lieutenant J. Hamilton (hired) : Taken by a French privateer and fome Dutch gun-boats in the Ems, November.

THUNDER, (Bb.) 8, F. Newcombe : Carried into Bilboa, in Spain, by mutiny of the crew, December.

PRIVATEERS.

PRIVATEERS,

FRENCH, DUTCH, and SPANISH,

TAKEN or DESTROYED by the BRITISH since the COMMENCEMENT of the WAR in 1793.

FRENCH PRIVATEERS TAKEN OR DESTROYED.

1793.

Names, Force in Guns, and Men.				By whom, where, and when, taken.
	Guns.	Swiv.	Men.	
Le Patriote	—	—	24	Childers, (floop,) 8, R. Barlow, near Gravelines, Feb. 15.
L'Elizabeth	—	—	—	Iphigenia, 32, P. Sinclair, in the Channel, Feb. 16.
L'Entreprenant . . .	—	—	—	Juno, 32, S. Hood, in the Channel, Feb. 17.
Le Sans Peur	—	—	—	Alligator, 28, W. Affleck, North Sea, Feb. 1.
Le Prend Tout . . .	—	—	—	Ditto. Feb. 21.
La Jeune Marie . . .	2	4	39	Ferret, (floop,) 12, W. Nowell, North Sea, Feb. 21.
Le Jean Bart	6	4	37	Ditto, Feb. 21.
Le Cuftine	—	8	24	Savage, (floop,) 16, A. Frafer, North Sea, Feb. 24.
(Name unknown) fch.	4	10	60	Hinde, (floop.) Feb.
Europa	—	—	—	Swan, 14, (revenue-cutter,) Channel, Feb.
La Marie Anne . . .	—	—	—	Ditto, Feb.
L'Affrique, cutter . .	—	—	—	Spitfire, (floop,) 14, P. C. Durham, Channel, Feb.
(Name unkn.) row-b.	4	0	22	Greyhound, (revenue-cutter,) in the Channel, Feb.
(Name unknown) .	—	—	18	Stag, (revenue-cutter,) in the Channel, Feb.

(Name

Names, Force in Guns, and Men	Guns.	Swiv.	Men	By whom, where, and when, taken.
(Name unkn.)row-b.	—	—	12	For une, (floop,) 16, F. Wooldridge, near Boulogne, Feb.
Le Cuftine, brig ..	—	—	—	Hind, 28, A. F. Cochrane, in the Channel, Feb.
(Name unkn.) boat,	—	—	9	Deal-boats, carried into Ramfgate, Feb.
L'Aftif, 30 tons ..	—	—	30	Greyhound, (revenue-cutter,) in the Channel, Feb.
La Palme	12	0	60	Juno, 32, S. Hood, in the Channel, March 2.
Sans Culottes....	—	12	22	Spider, (cutter,) 12, W. Lanyon, Channel, March 5.
L'Outade, brig ..	12	—	—	Tifiphone, (floop,) 12, in the Channel, March 5.
Le Cuftine	8	—	—	Iris, 32, G. Lumfdaine, North Sea, March 6.
Jean Bart	6	0	45	Falcon, (floop,) 14, J. Biffett, near Scilly, March 9.
Sans Culottes....	12	0	82	Scourge, (floop,) 16, G. Brifac, Channel, March 13.
Le Triton	—	—	—	Deftroyed by Childers, (floop,) 14, R. Barlow, March 14.
L'Hirondelle	16	0	85	Bofton, 32, G. W. A. Courtney, North Sea, March 20.
Les Trois Amis, boat,	4	0	25	Lizard, 28, T. Williams, and Cleopatra, 32, A. J. Ball, North Sea, March 24.
St. Jean, 8 tons ..	—	—	—	Spitfire, (floop,) 14, P. C. Durham, Channel, March.
St. Marguerite ...	—	—	—	Burnt, near Havre de Grace, by Ditto, March.
L'Aimable Marie .	10	—	—	Hind, 28, A. F. Cochrane, in the Channel, March.
Sans Culottes . , .	8	0	43	Lizard, 28, T. Williams, North Sea, March.
Le Vaillant Cuftine .	4	10	39	Ditto, March.
Malberfes	2	0	27	Swan, (revenue-cutter,) off Portland, March.
L'Amérique	—	—	32	Latona, 38, E. Thornbrough, off Bolthead, March.
L'Aimab. Liberté,lg.	—	—	20	Phaëton, 38, Sir A. S. Douglas, Channel ftation, March.
(Name unknown) .	—	—	17	Swan, (revenue-cutter,) off the Start-Point, March.
Le Jeune Benjamin .	4	0	40	Alarm, (revenue-lugger,) and Mary, (privateer,) and fent into Dartmouth, March.
Le Gen. Dumourier,	20	0	200	St. George, 98, Rear-Adm. J. Gell, Capt. T. Foley; Egmont, 74, A. Dickfon; Ganges, 74, A. J. P. Molloy; Edgar, 74, A. Bertie; Phaëton, 38, Sir A. S. Douglas off Cape Finifterre, April 14.
La Fantaifie	8	0	43	Ferret, (floop,) 14, W. Nowell, North Sea, fent into Deal, April 13.
L'Enfant de la Patrie,	10	0	28	Alarm, 32, J. Robertfon, and Swallow, (revenue-cutter,) fent into Shoreham, April 27.
Le Chauvelin ...	10	0	54	Alarm, 32, J. Robertfon, fent into the Downs, April 27.
Laborieux	—	—	—	L'Aimable, 32, Sir H. Burrard, and Juno, 32, S. Hood, in the Channel.
Le Republicain ...	6	0	37	Royal Charlotte, (Excife-cutter,) fent to Leith, April.
(Name unknown) lug.	6	0	60	Swallow (revenue-lugger,) fent into Portfmouth, April.
Le Cuftine, 50 tons,	6	7	47	Greyhound, (revenue-cutter,) fent into Weymouth, April.

(Name

Names, Force in Guns, and Men. Guns.Swiv.Men.	By whom, where, and when, taken.
(Name unknown) . 14 0 70	Ann, of Liverpool. and fent into Liverpool, April.
Le Taquin, brig . . 16 — —	Hind, 28, A. F. Cochrane, in the Channel,. April.
La Liberté. 12 0 55	Ditto, fent into Limerick, April.
L'Egalité 8 0 50	Ditto, fent into Limerick, April.
Sans Culottes . . . 16 — —	La Nymphe, 36, Sir E. Pellew ; and Venus, 32, J Faulknor ; fent into Falmouth, May 24.
Le Courier . . . . 10 16 —	L'Aimable, 32, Sir H. Burrard, and Circe, 28, J. St Yorke, in the Channel, May 26.
General Wafhington, 20 0 180	Tartar, 28, T. F. Fremantle, and Mermaid, 32, J. Trigge, Mediterranean ftation, May 27.
L'Angelique . . . 16 — —	Mermaid, 32, J. Trigge, Mediterranean ftation, May 30.
(Name unkn.) lug. 10 — —	Mary, Mollyneux, of Liverpool, fent to Hoy-Lake, May,
Franklin, brig . . . 10 — —	Latona, 38, E. Thornbrough, in the Channel, May.
La Georgette . . . . 20 — —	Hind, 28, A. F. Cochrane, fent into Falmouth, May.
Le Supreme 6 0 29	Dolphin, (revenue-cutter,) fent into Marazion, May
L'Augufte . . . . . 18 — —	Circe, 28, J. S. Yorke, in the Channel, May.
La Didon . . . . . . 14 — —	Ditto, May.
L'Ambitieux, lug. . 10 — —	Latona, 38, E. Thornbrough, in the Channel, May.
(Name unknown) . 10 — —	Captor unknown, off Lundy-Ifland, in Briftol Channel, fent into Padftow, May.
Le Guidelon 20 0 150	Boyne, 98, W. A. Otway, in the Channel,. June 1.
Le Robert 16 8 170	Syren, 32, J. Manley, in the Channel, June 13.
Club de Cherbourg, cutter . . . . . . } 10 — —	Crefcent, 36, J. Saumarez ; Hind, 28, A. F. Cochrane ; and Lively (privateer) ; between Breft and Ireland, June 22.
La Petite Victoire . — — —	Ceres, 32, R. Incledon ; and Nimble, (cutter,) 14, J. Smith ; North Sea.
Le Furet . . . . . . 14 — —	Trial, (cutter,) 12, Lieut. M. Malbon, North Sea, June 28.
L'Efpérance . . . . 12 — —	Druid, 32, J. Ellifon, in the Channel, June.
L'Oifeau, lug. 50 T. 6 0 50	Lottery, (cutter,) privateer, off Bellifle, June.
L'Efpoir . . . . . . 12 . 0 140	Crefcent,. 36,. Sir J. Saumarez-and Hind 28, A. F. Cochrane, in the Channel, June.
Le Poiffon Volant . 10 — —	Phaëton, 38, Sir A. S. Douglas, and Weazle, (floop,) 12, W. Taylor, in the Channel,- June.
Gen. Wafhington . . — — —	Ditto, June.
Phœnix . . . . . . 12 — —	Flora, 36, Sir.J. BoloVarreir, fent into Lifbon, June.
(Name unknown) . 14 — —	Caftor, 32, T. Trowbridge, and Mermaid, 32, J. Trigge, Mediterranean ftation,- June.

Lı

Names, Force in Guns, and Men.	Guns.	Swiv.	Men.	By whom, where, and when, taken.
La République Françoife . . .	—	—	—	Flora, 36, Sir J. B. Warren, in the Channel, June.
(Name unkn.) brig,	—	—	—	Falcon, (floop,) J. Biffett, off Portland, July.
L'Ami de Planteur, brig	14	0	90	Queen and Surprife, (privateer,) fent to Guernfey, July.
Le Paffe Partout . .	16	—	—	Thought, (privateer,) fent to Falmouth, July.
(Name unknown) .	8	0	72	Tarleton, Gilbody, and Eliza, Cannay, (letter of marque,) of Liverpool, July.
Le Vrai Patriote . .	—	—	—	Leviathan, 74; Coloffus, 74; and others; Mediterranean, July.
Le Sans Culottes . .	—	—	—	Orion, 74; J. T. Duckworth, coaft of America, Aug. 25.
Le Sans Pareil . . .	—	—	—	An Englifh frigate, coaft of Norway, Auguft.
Le Courier	—	—	—	Trimmer, (floop,) 16, F. Fayerman, and Liberty, (brig,) 16, J. C. Seaile, Auguft.
Le Patriote	—	—	—	Squirrel, W. O'B. Drury, and Liberty, (brig,) 16, J. C. Searle, Auguft.
Le Vengeur	—	—	—	Blanche, 32, C. Parker, Weft Indies, Oct. 1.
La Petite Zombi . .	—	—	—	Sea-Flower, (cutter,) 14, J. Webber, African ftation, Oct. 5.
La Révolution . . .	—	—	—	Blanche, 32, C. Parker, Weft Indies, Oct. 8.
Sans Culottes	20	—	—	Ditto, Dec. 28.

1794.

Le Vengeur	—	—	—	Rofe, 28, E. Riou, Weft Indies, Feb. 18.
La Guillotine . . .	10	—	—	Scorpion, (floop,) 16, T. Weftern, America, Aug. 2.
La Montagne . . .	—	—	—	Terpfichore, 32, R. Bowen, Weft Indies, Aug. 16.

1795.

Républicain Pageft .	—	—	—	Intrepid, 64, Hon. C. Carpenter, Weft Indies, } January and February.
Sans Pareil	—	—	—	Ditto,
Perroux	—	—	—	Ditto,
La Cocarde Nationale,	14	6	80	Lynx, (floop,) 16, J. P. Beresford, America, March 1.
(Name unkn.) brig,	16	0	75	Solebay, 32, fent into Barbadoes, March.
La Société	—	—	—	Swan, (floop,) T. Pearfe, Jamaica ftation, April 1.
La Spartiate, fch. .	—	—	—	Beaulieu, 40, E. Riou, Weft Indies, April 14.
(Name unkn.) fmall,	—	—	—	Blanche, 32, C. Sawyer, near St. Lucia, April 17.

La

Names, Force in Guns, and Men	Guns	Swiv	Men	By whom, where, and when, taken.
La Victoire	18	—	—	Scorpion, (sloop,) 16, T. Western, West Indies, April 19.
(Name unknown) .	—	—	—	Resource, 28, F. Watkins, West Indies, April.
L'Egalité	—	—	—	Scorpion, (sloop,) 16, T. Western, West Indies, May 8.
La Bellone, sch. . .	—	—	—	Bellona, 74, G. Wilson, West Indies, May 11.
La Rasoir Nationale,	6	—	—	Mosquito, (schooner,) 10, Lieutenant J. B. M'Farlane, Cuba, May.
La Resource République . . . . }	—	—	—	Cormorant, (sloop,) 16, J. Bingham, Jamaica, June 30.
Le Sans Pareil . . .	—	—	—	Scorpion, (sloop,) 16, T. Western, West Indies, July 22.
Le Républicain . .	—	—	—	Ditto, August 3.
L'Hirondelle	—	—	—	Ditto, August 7.
Le Poisson Volant, brig . . . }	—	—	—	Success, 32, H. Pigot, Jamaica station, September 30.
Grand Voltigeur, sch.	8	0	66	Hannibal, 74, J. Markham, West Indies, October 21.
La Convention . . .	12	0	74	Hannibal, 74, J. Markham, West Indies, October 24.
Petit Tonnerre, sch.	—	—	—	Hannibal, 74, J. Markham, West Indies, November 13.
L'Eléonore	—	—	—	Ferret, (sloop,) 14, C. Ekins, North Sea, November 20.
Le Petit Créole . .	—	—	—	Cormorant, (sloop,) 16, J. Bingham, Jamaica, Nov. 27.
Le Petit Peareu . .	6	0	42	Repulse, 64, W. G. Fairfax, coast of Holland, Dec. 3.
(Name unkn.) sch.	8	0	56	Pelican, (sloop,) 18, J. C. Searle, at Mariegalante, December 14.
La Desirée	—	—	—	Spider, (cutter,) 12, W. Lanyon.

1796.

	Guns	Swiv	Men	
La Vengeance . . .	—	—	—	Cormorant, (sloop,) 16, F. Collingwood, Jamaica station, January 19.
Gen. Rigaud	8	0	45	Favourite (sloop,) 16, J. A. Wood, at Trinidad, February.
(Name unkn.) small,	—	—	—	Ditto, (formerly the Hind packet,) February.
Banan	—	—	—	Destroyed by ditto, February.
(Name unknown) .	—	—	—	Alarm, 32, G. Vaughan ; and Zebra, (sloop,) 16 ; at Trinidad, February.
L'Aurore	—	—	—	Cleopatra, 32, C. V. Penrose, Halifax station, March 3.
(Name unknown) .	14	—	—	Favourite, (sloop,) 16, J. A. Wood, near Grenada, (formerly Susanna, of Liverpool,) March 9.
Lacedemonian, brig,	14	0	90	La Pique, 38, D. Milne ; and Charon, 44, J. Stevenson ; near Barbadoes, March 9.
L'Aspic	—	—	—	Quebec, 32, J. Cook, Channel, March 10.

F   Le

Names, Force in Guns, and Men.	Guns.	Swiv.	Men.	By whom, where, and when, taken.
Le Sans Peur, cutter,	8	—	—	La Pomone, 44, Sir J. B. Warren, and others, coaſt of France, March 13.
Le Courier	14	—	—	Porcupine, 24, J. Draper, Channel, March 20.
(Name unknown) .	—	—	—	Alarm, 32, G. Vaughan, and a ſloop, Gulf of Paria, — February or March.
(Name unknown) .	—	—	—	Ditto,
(Name unknown) .	—	—	—	Ditto,
L'Alexandre	10	0	66	Invincible, 74, W. Cayley, on a voyage to the Weſt Indies, April 1.
Le Furet *(long muſ-quetry)*	—	—	13	Racoon, (ſloop,) 16, E. Roe, coaſt of France, April.
(Name unknown) .	8	20	—	Agamemnon, 64, Commodore H. Nelſon, and others, off Loana, in the Mediterranean, April.
Le Petit Diable . .	—	—	—	Admiral Duncan's ſquadron, coaſt of Norway, April.
Le Poiſſon Volant, ſch.	—	—	—	L'Eſpérance, 22, J. Roſe, coaſt of America, *(formerly Flying-Fiſh,)* May 5.
Le Pichegru	10	0	34	Rattler, (ſloop,) 16, J. Cochet; and Diamond, 38, T. Le M. Goſſelin : off Cherbourg, May 6.
L'Epervier, lug. . .	2	6	26	Flora, (armed cutter,) 14, Lieutenant J. Reddy, off Dunkirk, May 14.
Le Hazard	—	—	—	Fairy, (ſloop,) 16, J. Irwin ; Reſolution, 10, (hired lug.) W. Chapman ; and Racoon, (ſloop,) 16, E. Roe ; in the Channel, May 22.
La Fantaiſie	14	0	75	La Pomone, 44, Sir J. B. Warren, and others, near Morlaix, May 25.
(Name unkn.) ſch.	4	—	—	Pelican, (ſloop,) 18, J. C. Searle, at St. Lucia, May 26.
(Name unknown) .	8	2	—	Ditto, May 26.
La Revanche, brig, *(pierced for 14 g.)*	12	0	85	La Suffiſante, 14, N. Tomlinſon, coaſt of France, May 27
Le Patriote	—	—	—	La Suffiſante, 14, N. Tomlinſon, coaſt of France, June 9
L'Eveille	6	0	100	La Trompeuſe, 18, J. R. Watſon, Iriſh coaſt, June 12.
Morgan, brig . . .	16	10	50	La Suffiſante, 14, N. Tomlinſon, French coaſt, June 28.
Leo	—	—	—	Raiſonable, 64, C. Boyles, Weſt Indies, June.
Le Milanie	—	—	—	Stately, 64, B. Douglas ; Rattleſnake, (ſloop,) 16, E. Ramage ; and Echo, (ſloop,) 16, J. Turner ; Cape of Good Hope, July 7.
La Revanche	18	0	167	Melpomene, 44, Sir C. Hamilton, near Breſt, July 11.
Le Terrible	14	—	—	Hazard, (ſloop,) 16, A. Ruddach, near Cape Clear, July 16.
Sans Culottes . . .	—	—	—	Roſe, (cutter,) ſent into Swanage, July.

Calvados,

Names, Force in Guns, and Men.	Guns	Swiv.	Men.
Calvados, cutter . .	6	10	83
La Marguerétta . .	4	0	40
L'Entreprife	—	—	—
(Name unknown,) fwivels only . .	—	—	17
L'Auguftine, fch. .	6	4	35
La Rockellaife, fch.	8	0	40
Le Brave, cutter . .	1	2	25
La Furet, lug. . . .	—	5	27
Le Requin	—	4	22
Le Petit Diable, 6 tons	—	—	14
L'Indemnité, brig; (pierced for 14 guns)	10	0	68
(Name unknown,) lug. fwivel arms,	—	—	20
Le Thurot, cutter .	4	6	25
La Victoire, fch. . .	6	4	65
(Name unknown,) 20 tons, f. arms,	—	—	18
La Bonne Efpérance	—	2	25
L'Iris	6	0	50
La Taupe à l'Œil, brig	8	0	42
Active, cutter . . .	6	0	23
Phœnix, cutter . .	4	0	32
(Name unknown,) fmall	—	—	—

By whom, where, and when, taken.

Cerberus, 32, J. Drew; and Seahorfe, 38; Irifh ftation, July.

Telemachus, (hired cutter,) 14, Lieutenant Crifpo, near Spithead, Auguft 5.

Duke of York, (excife-cutter,) J. Sarmon, Channel, Auguft 10.

Lion, (hired cutter,) 10, N. Symonds, off Beachy-Head, Auguft 16.

Difpatch, (Ruffian floop,) Ignateaff, off the Texel, Aug. 20.

Alcmene, 32, W. Brown, and others, on their paffage to the Mediterranean, Auguft 20.

Speedwell, (cutter,) 14, Lieutenant E. Williams, off St. Catharine's Point, Auguft 22.

Fly, (floop,) 16, R. H. Moubray, off Portland, Auguft 22.

Telemachus, (hired cutter,) 14, Lieutenant Crifpo, near the Ifle of Wight, Auguft 27.

Swallow, (revenue-cutter,) Amos, off Fairleigh, Aug. 27.

Diana, 38, J. Faulknor; Cerberus, 32, J. Drew; and Seahorfe, 38, G. Oakes; Irifh ftation, Auguft 28.

Antelope, (revenue-cutter,) Cafe, near Portland, Sept. 11.

Lion, (hired cutter,) 10, N. Symonds, near Beachy-Head, September 12.

Zebra, (floop,) 16, J. Hurft, between Grenada and Tobago, September 12.

Argus, (revenue-cutter,) North Sea, September 13.

Childers, (floop,) 14, S. Poyntz, off Cape Barfleur, September 14.

L'Aimable, 32, off Guadaloupe, September 15.

Penguin, (floop,) 18, J. K. Pulling, Irifh ftation, Sept. 18.

Racoon, (floop,) 16, E. Roe, off Dungenefs, Sept. 29.

Sylph, (brig,) 18, J. C. White, Channel, September.

Stag, (revenue-cutter,) fent into Haftings, September.

La

52   FRENCH PRIVATEERS

Names, Force in Guns, and Men.	Guns	Swiv.	Men.
La Revanche, fch.	12	0	75
Le Vautour, brig . .	9	0	78
Le Capit. Généreux, fch.	1	3	25
L'Entreprife	6	0	40
Le Buonaparte . . .	16	0	137
Le Vengeur	18	0	110
La Marie Anne, cut.	6	—	—
Providence, lug. . . (pierced for 8 guns,)	4	0	29
Le Franklin	12	0	100
L'Hirondelle, cutter,	10	0	60
Le Hardi Mendi- cant, cutter . .	—	—	—
L'Efpoir, lug. . . .	2	0	18
Le Hazard, cutter .	2	2	17
Le Sphinx, fmall arms	—	—	26
L'Hirondelle,(pier- ced for 16 guns,)	12	0	70
L'Aventure, brig .	16	0	62
Le Coup d'Effai, cut- ter	2	fw.	28
Maria	6	0	68
L'Efpérance, brig .	—	—	—
Maria Topaze . . .	10	0	64
La Didon, cutter . .	4	fw.	30
Les Deux Amis . .	14	0	80
La Mufette	22	0	150
La Legere, fch. . .	6	0	48
LaRefléché (pierced for 14 guns) . . .	12	0	67

By whom, where, and when, taken.

Indefatigable, 38, Sir E. Pellew, and others, off Breft, October 2.
Dryad, 36, Lord Beauclerc, Irifh ftation, October 16.
Adventure, (S. S.) 44, G. W. Rutherford, and another, Weft Indies, October 18.
Unicorn, 32, Sir T. Williams, Irifh Channel, October 21.
Sta Margaritta, 36, T. B. Martin, Irifh ftation, Oct. 24.
Ditto, October 25.
Dover, (hired cutter,) 12, Lieutenant W. Sharp, in the Channel, October.
Ditto, October.
Artois, 38, Sir E. Nagle, and others, Channel, Nov. 2.
Cerberus, 32, J. Drew, Irifh ftation, November 5.
Phœnix, (hired cutter,) 10, H. Pafcall, near Orfordnefs, November 20.
Marfhal de Cobourg, (hired cutter,) Lieutenant C. Webb, off Dungenefs, December 12.
Lion, (hired cutter,) N. Symonds, near Spithead, Dec. 14.
Eurydice, 24, J. Talbot, North Sea, December 15.
Cleopatra, 32, Vice-Admiral Murray, on the paffage from Hallifax to England, Dec 16.
Greyhound, 32, J. Young, off Cape Barfleur, Dec. 19.
Star, (floop,) 18, Hon. J. Colvill, off the Ifle of Wight, December 20.
La Minerve, 42, G. Cockburn, near Sardinia, Dec. 23.
Diamond, 38, Sir R. Strachan, near Alderney, Dec. 24.
Lapwing, 28, R. Barton, off Montferrat, December 28.
Cerberus, 32, J. Drew, in the Channel, December 29.
Polyphemus, 64, G. Lumfdaine; and Apollo, 38, J. Manley; Irifh ftation, December.

1797.

Hazard, (floop,) 16, A. Ruddoch, Irifh ftation, Jan 1.
Bellona, 74, G. Wilfon, near Defeada, January 7.
Zephyr, (floop,) 14. R. Lawrie, on the paffage to Barbadoes, January 8.

(Name

Names, Force in Guns, and Men.	Guns	Swiv	Men	By whom, where, and when, taken.
(Name unknown,) fch.	—	—	—	Bellona, 74, G. Wilfon; and Babet, 20, W. G. Lobb; driven on-fhore on Defeada, January 10.
I.'Eclair	18	0	120	Unicorn, 32, Sir T. Williams, Channel, January 11.
La Molinette, fch..	—	2	18	Swallow, (brig,) 18, G. Fowke, near Bahamas, Jan. 27.
L'Efpoir, fch. ...	4	10	48	Lapwing, 28, R. Barton, off Barbuda, January 31.
La Favorite	8	0	60	Lord Bridport's fleet, in the Channel, January.
La Liberté, lug...	3	4	18	Griffin, (hired cutter,) B. Fifk, North Sea, January.
Le Cotentin	—	—	—	Harpy, (floop,) 18, H. Bazely, in the Channel; February.
Le Sans Peur, cutter,	—	2	18	Syren, 32, T. Le M. Goffelin, off Cherbourg, February 2.
LeRequin,flp,mufq.	—	—	20	Lion, (hired cutter,) 10, N. Symonds, off Dungenefs, February 3.
Le Flibuftier, lug..	14	6	63	Eurydice, 24, J. Talbot, and others, North Sea, Feb. 6.
LaJeuncEmilie,brig,	10	0	62	Triton, 32, J. Gore, and others, Channel, February 11.
Recovery, cutter..	14	0	46	Ditto, February 11.
La Difficile	18	0	206	Ditto, February 12.
Le Buonaparte ...	17	0	110	L'Efpion, 38, M. Dixon; and Martin, (floop,) 16, S, Sutton; North Sea, February 14.
La Tartane, brig..	16	0	60	Greyhound, 32, J. Young, near Beachy-Head, Feb. 18.
Le Victorieux ...	4	0	30	Leopard, 50, W. Hargood, near Scarborough, Feb. 18.
Le Furet	10	0	50	Scourge, (floop,) 16, H. R. Glynn, Channel, Feb. 21.
L'Appocrate, brig.	14	0	65	Stag, 32, J. S. Yorke, near Scilly, February 21,
L'Hirondelle, cutter,	6	0	45	Ditto, deftroyed, February 21.
L'Aventure, f. 40 tons, pift. ...	—	—	11	Swift, (cutter,) 10, Lieutenant Sir J. Colleton, near the South Foreland, February 24.
Le Mandarin	—	—	—	Hind, (hired cutter,) 14, Lieutenant Woodcock; and Telemachus, (hired cutter,) Lieut. Newton; in the Channel, February 24.
(Name unknown) .	—	—	—	Burnt at the capture of Trinidad, February.
La Fortune	8	0	74	Magicienne, 32, W. H. Ricketts, ⎫
Le Poiffon Volant.	12	0	80	Ditto, ⎪ Jamaica ftation, be-
Le Poiffon Volant.	5	0	50	Ditto, ⎬ tween January and
La Fougoufe	6	0	57	Diligence, (brig,) 16, ⎪ March.
(Name unkn.) fch.	—	—	—	Boats of fquadron on ⎭
L'Actif	18	0	120	Phaëton, 38, Hon. R. Stopford, Channel, March 6,
Le Surveillant ...	16	0	160	Alcmene, 32, W. Brown, Irifh Coaft, March 6.
La Liberté Générale,	—	—	—	Mermaid, 32, R. W. Otway, Jamaica ftation, March 7.
L'Impromptu,cutter,	4		31	Nimble, (cutter,) 14, Lieutenant Festing, off St, Aldan's Head, March 7.

Le

Names, Force in Guns, and Men.	Guns.	Swiv.	Men.	By whom, where, and when, taken.
Le Bonheur, cutter,	2	2	24	Nimble, (cutter,) 14, Lieut. Fefting, off the Ifle of Wight, March 7.
Le Voltigeur, lug. . —	fw.		23	Eurydice, 24, J. Talbot, off the Flemifh Banks, March 7.
L'Heureufe Catha- riné, fch.	6	0	51	Lapwing, 28, R. Barton, off St. Chriftopher's, March 7.
Le Vautour, cutter, mufq.	—	—	28	L'Impétueux, 78, J. W. Payne, and óthers, in the Channel, March 8.
Paжt au Paix, fch. . —		2	17	Swallow, (floop,) 18, G. Fowke, Cape Nicolas Mole, March 11.
La Cafca	6	0	50	Bittern, (floop,) 16, J. Lavie, off Barbadoes, March 15.
L'Epervier, floop .	4	3	29	Plymouth, (hired lugger,) 14, Lieut. R. Elliott, near the Start Point, March 21.
La Liberté, lug. . . —		—	18	Greyhound, (revenue-cuttèr,) Wilkinfon, near Cape Barfleur, March 21.
(Name unknown) . —		—	—	Burnt in a harbour in Porto Rico by the Hermione, 32, H. Pigot, March 22.
(Name unknown) . —		—	—	
(Name unknown) . —		—	—	
Le Buonaparte, cutter	14	—	—	La Suffifante, 14, J. Wittman, in the Channel, March 25.
Le Neptune	16	0	90	Aurora, 28, H. Digby, Weft of Cape Finifterre, March 27.
L'Amitié, fch. . .	14	0	55	Plymouth, (hired Lugger,) Lieut. Elliott, near Alderney, March 29.
Le Général, brig, (pierced for 18 guns)	14	0	104	King's Fifher, (floop,) 18, J. Bligh, near Oporto, March 29.
Le Hardi, brig . . .	18	0	130	Hazard, (floop,) 16, A. Ruddach, near the Skellocks, Ireland, April 1.
Les Bons Amis . .	6	0	32	Spitfire, (floop,) 20, M. Seymour, off the Eddiftone, April 2.
Le Prend Garde à Loup	2	fw.	28	Dover, (hired cutter,) 12, Lieut. Sharp, off the Lizard, April 3.
Le Poiffon Volant .	4	0	40	Tamer, 38, T. B. Martin, Weft Indies, April 4.
Le Chaffeur	6	0	80	L'Aimable, 32, W. G. Lobb, off Guadaloupe, April 6.
La Sophie, cutter .	14	0	40	Kangaroo, (floop,) 18, Hon. C. Boyle, near the Lizard, April 9.
Le Voltigeur, fch. .	8	8	40	Veftal, 28, C. White, North Sea, April 10.
L'Incroyable	24	0	220	Flora, 36, R. G. Middleton, and Pearl, 32, S. J. Ballard, on the paffage, between Lifbon and England, April 13.

L'Enfant

Names, Force in Guns, and Men.	Guns.	Swiv.	Men.	By whom, where, and when, taken.
L'Enfant de la Patrie	16	0	130	Boston, 32, J. N. Morris, off Cape Finisterre, April 16.
Les Amis, cutter .	2	6	31	Racoon, (sloop,) 18, R. Lloyd, North Sea, April 20.
La Petite Hélene, lug.	2	0	33	La Suffisante, 14, J. Wittman, in the Chánnel, April 21.
Daphne	2	2	25	Nancy, (revenue-cutter,) R. Willis, near the Isle of Wight, April 26.
L'Espérance, cutter,	—	—	—	Diamond, 38, Sir R. Strachan, near Cape La Heve, Apr. 27.
Le Basque, brig ..	8	0	50	Indefatigable, 44, Sir E. Pellew, and others, in the Channel, April 30.
L'Aimable Manet. brig	14	0	69	Spitfire, (sloop,) 20, M. Seymour, in the Channel, May 1.
La Bayonaise, sch. .	2	sw	36	Cyane, 18, R. Manning, off Dominica, May 3.
LaNouvelleEugénie,	16	0	120	Indefatigable, 44, Sir E. Pellew, and others, in the Channel, May 11.
La Dunkerquoise .	18	0	100	Cerberus, 32, J. Drew, Irish station, May 11.
L'Espiègle, lugger, small arms ...	—	—	30	La Melpomene, 44, Sir C. Hamilton, near the Isle of Wight, May 15.
Le Flibustier	14	0	70	Spider, (schooner,) 14, Lieut. D. Dent, off the Lizard, May 16.
L'Espiègle, lug. ..	4	0	36	Phœnix, 36, L. W. Halsted, near Waterford, May 18.
La Jalouse, sch. ..	4	0	45	Tamer, 38, T. B. Martin, off Antigua, May 20.
Le Terrible, lug. ..	4	0	25	Penguin, (sloop,) 18, J. K. Pulling, off the Lizard, May 24.
La Galatée, sch. ..	8	0	55	Tamer, 38, T. B. Martin, off Antigua, May 28.
La Trompeuse, sch.	6	0	40	Spitfire, (sloop,) 20, M. Seymour, in the Channel, May.
La Justine Adelaide, lug.	2	2	20	Pilote, (brig,) 14, Lieut. W. Compton, in the Channel, May.
L'Adolph, lug. ..	12	8	35	Nautilus, (sloop,) 16, H. Gunter, and others, May.
La Liberté, sch. ..	6	0	13	Proselyte, 32, J. Loring, West Indies, } Between
Le Buonaparte, sch.	3	0	35	Ambuscade, 32, T. Twyfden, West Indies, } April and
Gén. Touffaint, sch.	8	0	5	Swallow, (brig,) 18, G. Fowke, West Indies, } June.
(Name unkn.) lug.	2	8	36	Dolphin, (revenue-cutter,) John, near Mount's Bay, June 1.
L'Unité, lug. ...	14	0	58	St. Fiorenzo, 40, Sir H. B. Neale, off the Owers, June 3.
Le Pichegru, brig .	1	sw.	39	Resolution, (brig,) 14, Lieut. Huggett, off the Start, June 3.
Flying-Fish, lug. .	—	2	24	Lively, (revenue-cutter,) D. Smith, North Sea, June 5.
Louis Bonfoi, sch. .	4	0	66	Lapwing, 28, R. Barton, off Barbuda, June 9.
L'Heureuse, sch. .	2	0	26	Tamer, 38, T. B. Martin, off Martinique, June 10.

La

Names, Force in Guns, and Men.	Guns.	Swiv.	Men.	By whom, where, and when, taken.
La Zoée	20	0	120	L'Impétueux, 78, J. W. Payne, and others, coaft of France, June 11.
Syrene, cutter	6	0	27	Naut lus, (floop,) 16, H. Gunter, and Fox, (cutter,) off Fleckerv, in Norway, June 12.
(Name unkn.) brig,	6	0	24	L'Aigle, 38, C. Tyler, coaft of Portugal, June 12.
Le Poiffon Volant, fch.	4	0	38	Tamer, 38, T. B. Martin, off Defeada, June 14.
Le Vengeur des François	4	0	35	Zephyr, (floop,) 14, Lt. Reynolds, off Dominica, June 18.
J.'Audacieux, lug.	1	2	46	Diligence, (revenue-cutter,) G. Hough, Channel, June 20.
L'Efpérance, row-boat	—	10	32	Harpy, (floop,) 18, H. Bazeley, coaft of France, June 22.
Le Triton, (pierced for 18 guns)	8	0	180	Magnanime, 44, Hon. M. De Courcy, 70 leagues weft of Cape Clear, June 22.
La Surprife, lug.	8	0	48	Kangaroo, (floop,) 18, Hon. C. Boyle, in lat. 46° north, long. 7° weft, June 22.
La Barbaroffa, fch.	8	0	61	Tamer, 38, T. B. Martin, off Defeada, Weft Indies, June 23.
L'Efpoir	—	2	15	Viper, (excife-cutter,) R. Adams, North Sea, June 24.
Flibuftier, brig	12	0	104	Maidftone, 32, J. Matthews, Weft Indies, June 24.
Le Poiffon Volant, lugger	14	0	50	Trent, 36, E. Bowater, near Yarmouth, June 27.
Tiger of Dunkirk, lugger	2	4	28	Repulfe, (revenue-cutter,) Munnings, off Orfordnefs, June 27.
Le Succès, lug.	6	0	42	Telemachus, (hired cutter,) 14, Lieut. Newton, in the Channel, June 28.
L'Argonaute, lug.	2	10	—	Galatea, 32, G. Byng, between Cape Clear and Scilly, June 30.
Caftor, lug.	14	0	57	St. Fiorenzo, 40, Sir H. B. Neale, 60 leagues weft of Scilly, July 1.
Les Graces, lug.	1	2	22	Viper, (excife-cutter,) R. Adams, near Harwich, July 2.
L'Actéon, cutter	6	0	30	Hamadryad, 36, T. Elphinftone, Straits of Gibraltar, July 3.
La Légere, fch.	6	0	50	Zephyr, (floop,) 14, Lieut. Reynolds, off Mariegalante, July 6.
Le Vétéran, floop	8	0	24	Lapwing, 28, R. Barton, to leeward of Montferrat, July 6.
Le Dorad, floop	4	0	74	Ditto to leeward of Montferrat, July 7.
Le Va-tout, fch.	2	0	32	Zephyr, (floop,) 14, Lieutenant Reynolds, off Martinique, July 8.

L'Adour,

Names, Force in Guns, and Men.	Guns.	Swiv.	Men.	By whom, where, and when, taken.
L'Adour, - (pierced for 20 guns) . .	16	0	147	Sta Margaritta, 36, G. Parker, 8 leagues from Cape Clear, July 10.
Le Du Guay Trouin,	22	0	127	Doris, ?6, Lord Ranelagh : and Galatea, 32, G. Byng; latitude 47° north, longitude 9° west, July 15.
Le Papillon . . . . —	4		30	Dolphin, (revenue-cutter,) R. Johns, Channel, July 19.
Le Profpéré, brig .	14	0	73	Tifiphone, (floop,) 20, R. Honeyman ; and Rambler (brig) ; on the Dogger-Bank, July 22.
La PetiteChérie, lug.	4	fw.	22	L'Impétueux, 78, J. W. Payne, near Muros-Bay, July 23.
Capt. Thurot, cutter,	2	4	22	Sea-Gull, (floop,) 18, H. Wray, and King George, (cutter,) near Chriftianfand, July 23.
Le Hardi, lug. . . .	4	0	30	Telemachus, (hired cutter,) Lieutenant T. Newton, off Cape La Hogue, July 24.
Le Poiffon Volant, brig, (pierced for 8 guns)	4	—	—	La Concorde, 36, B. Roberts, 40 leagues from Cape Finifterre, July 24.
Le. Courier de la Mer, brig . . .	12	0	20	Trial, (cutter,) 12, Lieutenant Garrett, near Portland, July 25.
Hazard, lug.	8	0	50	L'Aigle, 38, C. Tyler, and Bofton, 32, J. N. Morris, off Cape Finifterre, July 30.
(Name unkn.) lug.	2	0	25	Duke of York, (hired lugger,) 8, and Hind, (revenue-cutter,) in the Channel, July.
L'Incroyable	2	0	21	Hind, (revenue-cutter,) Murray, in the Channel, July.
L'Achéron	1	6	40	Beresfoid, (Irifh revenue-brig,) near Waterford, July.
Le Régulus, floop .	4	0	26	Lapwing, 28, R. Barton, northward of Tortola, Auguft 1.
Le Pont d'Arcol, cutter	4	0	48	Tamer, 38, T. B. Martin, off Mariegalante, Auguft 4.
Le Renard, cutter .	10	0	71	Ditto, off Martinique, Auguft 8.
La Victorine, fch. .	16	0	82	Sta Margaritta, 36, G. Parker, 90 leagues fouth-weft of Cape Clear, Auguft 8.
L'Utile	14	0	135	Tamer, 38, T. B Martin, off Barbadoes, Auguft 10.
La Marie Anne . .	14	0	90	Aurora, 28, H. Digby, Lifbon ftation, Auguft 13.
La Mouche, lug . .	8	8	49	L'Aigle, 38, C. Tyler, Lifbon ftation, Auguft 13.
La Prodigée, brig, (pierced for 18 guns)	14	0	87	L'Efpiègle, (floop,) 16, J. Boorder, North Sea, Auguft 14.
Le Lynx, lug. . . .	14	0	50	Stork, (floop,) 18, R. H. Péarfon, near the Humber, Auguft 15.
Le Tiercelet, fch. .	8	10	47	Magnanime, 44, Hon. M. De Courcy, Irifh ftation, Auguft 15.

Le

Names, Force in Guns, and Men.	Guns	Swiv.	Men.	By whom, where, and when, taken.
Le Coq	6	0	34	Alexander, (armed tender,) Lieutenant W. W. Senhoufe, Martinique, August 15.
L'Eclair, brig ...	14	0	108	Drvad, 36, Lord Beauclerc, Irish ftation, August 19.
La Revanche, lug. } (pierced for 10 g.) }	4	0	34	Refolution, (hired lugger,) 10, G. Broad; and others, North Sea, Auguft 19.
L'Oifeau, (pierced for 20 guns) .. }	18	0	119	Penguin, (floop,) 18, J. K. Pulling, Irifh ftation, Auguft 21.
La Victorieufe, lug.	1	5	22	L'Efpiegle, (floop,) 16, J. Boorder, off Holland, Aug. 27.
La Pluvier	9	0	43	La Bonne Citoyenne, (floop,) 20, R. Retalick, in the Mediterranean, Auguft.
La Canarde	10	0	64	Ditto, Auguft.
Le Furet, lug. ... —	4	17		Orcftes, (floop,) 18, C. Parker, off Portland, Sept. 3.
Le Cerf Volant, lug.	14	6	63	Tifiphone, 20, R. Honeymau, 5 leagues from Heligoland, September 6.
L'Aigle	12	0	77	Aurora, 28, H. Digby, Lifbon ftation, September 7.
Le Fabius	20	0	140	Doris, 36, Lord Ranelagh, Irifh ftation, September 8.
La Cornelie, brig .	12	0	90	Dryad, 36, Lord Beauclerc, Irifh ftation, funk, Sept. 9.
Le Neptune, cutter,	12	0	55	Diana, 38, J. Faulknor, and Cerberus, 32, J. Drew, Irifh ftation, September 12.
L'Agréable.....	18	0	115	Bittern, (floop,) 16, Lieutenant E. Kittoe, off Tortola, September 13.
L'Incroyable, fch. .	3	0	31	Spitfire, (floop,) 20, M. Seymour, 13 leagues fouth-weft from the Lizard, September 15.
L'Efpoir, lug. ...	2	4	39	King's Fifher, (floop,) 10, C. H. Pierrepont, off Camina, Lifbon ftation, September 15.
L'Efpiègle, brig ..	14	0	60	Aurora, 28, H. Digby, Lifbon ftation, September 15.
Le Chaffeur, fch. .	6	0	47	Phaeto 38, Hon. R. Stopford, and others, in the Channel, September 16.
La Brunette, brig, (pierced for 16 guns) }	10	0	80	L Unité, 38, C. Rowley, near L'Iile de Dieu, September 17.
La Trompeufe, fch.	12	0	78	Pelican, (brig,) 18, Lieutenant White, and Drake. (floon.) 14, J Perkins, Jamaica ftation, funk. September 17.
(Name unkn.) lug. — —	—			Diamond, 38, Sir R. Strachan, near Cape La Heve, deftroyed, September 23.
Indian	16	—	—	Phaeton, 38, Hon. R. Stopford, and L'Unité, 38, C. Rowley, off the Roches Bonnes, September 24.
L'Entreprenant, cut.	1	fw.	23	Weazle, (floop,) 12, J. M. Lewis, off the Land's End, September 29.

La

Names, Force in Guns, and Men.	Guns.	Swiv.	Men.	By whom, where, and when, taken.
La Sarazine, fch. .	6	0	58	Scourge, 22, S. Warren, off Mariegalante, September 28.
Le Jean Bart, lug . —		8	24	Telemachus, (hired cutter,) 14, Lieutenant Newton, off Portland, September 29.
Le Cocyte, lug. . . .	4	0	30	Stag, 38, J. S. Yorke, off Plymouth, deftroyed, Sept. 30.
La Nantaife, fch. .	3	—	—	Albicore, (floop,) 16, S. P. Forfter,
(Name unkn.) barge,	1	—	—	Thames, 32, W. Lukin,
(Name unkn.) fch. .	2	fw.	30	Drake, (floop,) 14, J. Perkins,
(Name unkn) fch. .	1	0	20	Aquilon, 32, W. E. Cracraft,
(Name unk:) barge, armed	—	—	—	Rattler, (floop,) 16, J. Hall,
(Name unk.) barge, armed	—	—	—	Ditto,
(Name unk.) fch. .	3	0	56	Albicore, (floop,) 16, S. P. Forfter
(Name unk.) row-b. —		fw.	—	Ditto,

(Jamaica ftation, between Auguft and October.)

Names, Force in Guns, and Men.	Guns.	Swiv.	Men.	By whom, where, and when, taken.
L'Epicharis	8	0	74	Alexander, (armed tender,) Lieutenant W. W. Senhoufe, off Barbadoes, October 4.
Le Rayon, lug. . .	6	8	54	Melampus, 36, G. Moore, near the Cafket Lights, Oct. 5.
(Name unkn.) lug. —	—	—		Fairy, (floop,) 16, J. S. Horton, funk off Boulogne, October 5.
La Découverte . . . —	—	—		Phaëton, 38, Hon. R. Stopford ; Stag, 32, J S. Yorke ; and L'Unité, 24, C. Rowley ; Channel, October 7.
La Brune	16	0	180	Dryad, 36, Lord A. Beauclerc, and Doris, 32, Lord Ranelagh, Irifh ftation, October 10.
Les Amis, cutter .	2	2	18	Speedwell, (hired lugger,) 10, Lieutenant Tomlinfon, in the Channel, October 10.
Telemachus, lug. .	6	6	35	Speedwell, (hired lugger,) 10, Lieutenant Tomlinfon, near the Start, October 13.
La Perle	12	—	—	Pelican, (brig.) 18, Lieutenant White, Jamaica ftation, (formerly the Port-Royal fchooner) October 18.
Le Zephyr, brig . .	8	0	70	Boadicea, 30, R. G. Keats, and Anfon, 44, P. C. Darham, Channel ftation, October 19.
Le Furet, fch. (pierced for 14 guns) .	4	0	50	Triton, 32, J. Gore, and Childers, (floop,) 14, J. O'Bryen, near Ifle Bas, October 14.
L'Hyenne, (formerly Hyæna, taken from the Britifh in 1794)	24	0	230	Indefatigable, 44, Sir E. Pellew, near Teneriffe, Oct. 25.
Le Flibuftier, cutter,	4	5	29	Diana, 38, J. Faulknor, Irifh ftation, October.

L'Epervier

Names, Force in Guns, and Men.	Guns.	Swiv.	Men.	By whom, where, and when, taken.
L'Epervier (pierced for 20 guns)	16	0	145	Cerberus, 32, J. Drew, Irish station, November 12.
L'Epervier, lug.	2	4	25	Fairy, (sloop.) 16, J. S. Horton, and Fox, second, (cutter,) coast of France, November 13.
L'Emouchet, lug.	8	6	55	Albatrofs, (brig,) 18, G. Scott, 8 leagues from the Texe, November 14.
Le Renard (pierced for 20 guns)	18	0	189	Cerberus, 32, J. Drew, Irish station, November 14.
Le Railleur	20	0	160	Boadicea, 30, R. G. Keats, and Anson, 44, P. C. Durham, Channel station, November 17.
Le Coureur, brig	14	0	90	Blanche, 32, H. Hotham, Lisbon station, November 20.
La Marie, brig	14	0	60	Jason, 38, C. Stirling, off Belleisle, November 21.
(Name unk.) cutter,	—	—	—	Penelope, (cutter,) 18, Lieutenant Burdwood, off the Start, November 26.
L'Aigle, fch. (pierced for 14 guns)	12	0	62	Latona, 38, F. Sotheron, Lisbon station, November 29.
L'Aventure, fch.	3	0	43	Aurora, 28, H. Digby, near Cape Roxent, Lisbon station, November.
La Minerve	4	0	52	L'Aigle, 38, C. Tyler, Lisbon station, December 1.
L'Intrépide, brig (pierced for 18 guns)	15	0	83	Latona, 38, F. Sotheron, Lisbon station, December 3.
Le Dragon, fch.	12	0	80	Tamer, 38, C. Western, to windward of Barbadoes, December 4.
La Mouche (pierced for 22 guns)	16	0	122	Diana, 38, J. Faulknor, and Shannon, 32, A. Fraser, Irish station, December 5.
Le Dix-huit de Fructidor, floop,	10	0	75	Tamer, 38, C. Western, to windward of Barbadoes, December 7.
Le Succès, brig	—	—	—	Clyde, 38, C. Cunningham, Channel station, December 13.
La Dorade (pierced for 18 guns)	12	0	93	Ditto, December 15.
La Decidée, fch.	10	0	89	Alfred, 74, T. Totty, off Martinique, December 16.
L'Epervier, cutter	3	2	24	Ann, (cutter,) of Hastings, and another, off Alderney, December 24.
Le Delphine, cutter (pierced for 10 guns)	4	0	38	Niger, 32, E. Griffith, off the Start-Point, December 25.
Le Bayonnois, brig,	6	0	40	Blanche, 32, H. Hotham, Lisbon station, December 27.

Le

Names, Force in Guns, and Men.				By whom, where, and when, taken.
	Guns.	Swiv.	Men.	
Le Brutus	9	—	—	Magicienne, 32, W. H. Ricketts, and others, off Porto Rico, December 27.
La Victoire, fch. . .	14	0	74	Termagant, (floop,) 18, D. Lloyd, 4 leagues from the Spurn-Light, December 28.
Le Hazard, brig . .	14	—	—	Phaeton, 38, Hon. R. Stopford, Channel station, Dec. 28.
L Aventure	12	0	190	Mermaid, 32, J. Newman, 30 leagues from Belleifle, Dec. 31.
(Name unk.) fch. .	10	—	—	Jamaica, 26, S. Brooking, deftroyed,
La Fortunée, fch. .	2	—	—	Jamaica, 26, S. Brooking,
Le Petit Reſource .	1	2	—	Swallow, (brig.) 18, G. Fowke,
Le Créole, fch. . .	6	—	—	Ceres, 32, R. W. Otway,
(Name unkn.) fch.	—	—	—	Gannett, (cutter,)
(Name unkn.) fch.	—	—	—	Recovery. (fchooner,) 10, Lieut. W. Rofs,
La Magicienne . . .	16	—	—	Valiant, 74, J. Crawley, and others,
Le Bien Venu, fch.	8	—	—	Carnatic, 74, G. Bowen, (1,) and others (pierced for 14 guns),
Le Tartare	—	—	—	Childers, (floop,) 14, J. O'Bryen, in the Channel,
La Helene	—	—	—	Triton, 32, J. Gore, in the Channel,
Le Triton	—	—	—	La Melpomene, 44, Sir C. Hamilton, ditto,

Weſt Indies, between Oct. 1797, and March, 1798.

About the end of 1797.

1798.

L'Aventure	—	—	—	Phaëton, 38, Hon. R. Stopford, Channel station, Jan. 1.
Le Caye du Pont, fch.	16	0	129	La Concorde, 36, R. Barton, off St. Bartholomews, Jan. 3.
Le Requin	20	0	90	L'Aigle, 38, C. Tyler, Coaſt of Corunna, Jan. 4.
Le Vengeur, fch. . .	12	0	72	Indefatigable, 44, Sir E. Pellew; Cambrian, 44, A. K. Legge; and Childers, (floop,) 14, J. O'Bryan; in the Channel, Jan. 4.
Le Benjamin (pierced for 20 guns)	16	0	132	Mercury, 28, T. Rogers, and others, Liſbon ſtation, Jan. 5.
La Zelie	—	—	—	Stag, (hired cutter,) 14, Lieut. Worth, Channel, Jan. 5.
Buonaparte	2	fw.	40	Alcmene, 32, G. Hope, and others, Liſbon ſtation, Jan. 8.
La Betſey, (pierced for 20 guns) . .	16	0	118	King's Fiſher, (floop,) 18, C. H. Pierrepont, Liſbon ſtation, Jan. 8.
La Proferpine, fch. .	8	0	82	La Concorde, 36, R. Barton, off Montferrat, Jan. 8.
L'Intrigue, flp . . .	6	0	64	Lapwing, 28, T. Harvey, off Martinique, Jan. 9.
Le Policrate, cutter,	16	0	72	Racoon, (floop,) 18, R. Lloyd, Channel, Jan. 11.
L Emprunt Foſſe . .	2	6	25	La Pomone, 44, R. C. Reynolds, Channel, Jan. 11.
Le Henri, bg . . .	14	0	108	Gorgon, 44, R. Williams, Liſbon ſtation, Jan. 13.
Les Trois Sœurs, bg,	16	0	100	Mercury, 28, T. Rogers, Liſbon ſtation, Jan. 15 (pierced for 18 guns).

G   L'Incon-

Names, Force in Guns, and Men.	Guns.	Swiv.	Men.	By whom, where, and when, taken.
L'Inconcevable . .	8	0	55	Indefatigable, 44, Sir E. Pellew, and his fquadron, in the Channel, Jan. 16.
La Belliqueufe . . .	18	0	120	Melampus, 36, G. Moore ; and Seahorfe, 38, E. J. Foote ; Irifh coaft, January 16 *(pierced for 20 guns)*.
La Defirée, fch. . .	6	0	46	Boats of La Babet, 20, J. Mainwaring, Weft Indies, Jan. 16.
L'Heureux	—	—	—	} Thefeus, 74, R. W. Miller; Swiftfure, 74, A. Philip;
La Harmonie . . .	—	—	—	and others ; Lifbon ftation, Jan. 18.
Le Hypomené . . .	—	—	—	
La Cerès, *(pierced for 14 guns)* . .	2	0	45	Matilda, 24, H. Mitford, off Antigua, Jan. 19.
La Rencontre, flp . .	6	0	49	Alfred, 74, T. Totty, off Dominica, January 20.
La Penfée, fch. . . .	2	9	32	Racoon, (floop,) 18, R. Lloyd, Channel, Jan. 22.
La Volage	22	0	195	Melampus, 36, G. Moore, S. W. coaft of Ireland, Jan. 23.
Le Venturer, cutter, *(pierced for 8 guns)*	2	6	33	Penelope, (hired cutter,) 18, Lieut. Burdwood, 10 leagues from the Start, Jan. 24.
La Conftance, bg, *(pierced for 18 g.)*	12	0	96	Mercury, 28, T. Rogers, Lifbon ftation, Jan. 25.
L'HeureufeNouvelle,	22	0	133	Indefatigable, 44, Sir E. Pellew, and his fquadron, Jan. 28.
Four row-boats . .	—	fw.	—	By the different Cruifers in the Weft Indies, in the months of January and February, 1798.
Le Duguay Trouin .	24	0	150	Shannon, 32, A. Frafer, off Cape Clear, Feb. 2.
La Batterie Répub- lique, floop . . .	4	0	38	Amphitrite, 28, C. Ekins, off St. Lucia, Feb. 2.
Le Mars	16	0	222	Dryad, 36, Lord A. Beauclerc, 20 leagues from Cape Clear, February 4 *(pierced for 20 guns)*.
Antoine, bg . . .	16	0	70	Thalia, 36, Lord H. Paulet, Feb. 5.
L'Atout	—	—	—	Thalia, 36, Lord H. Paulet, and others, Lifbon ftation, Feb. 5.
Fortunée	—	—	—	Jamaica, 26, S. Brooking, Jamaica ftation, Feb. 7.
Le Jafon	12	0	108	Anfon, 44, P. C. Durham, Channel ftation, Feb. 8.
L'Efpoir, flp. . .	8	0	66	Zephyr, (floop,) 14, W. Champion, off Defeada, Feb. 8.
Le Hardi, fch. . .	8	0	60	La Concorde, 36, R. Barton, off Barbuda, Feb. 11.
Le Chaffeur Bafque, brig	8	0	72	Emerald, 36, T. M. Waller, Lifbon ftation, Feb. 12.
Le Hazard, fch. .	2	0	27	La Concorde, 36, R. Barton, off Montferrat, Feb. 13.
Le Mutine, fch. .	8	0	61	Lapwing, 28, T. Harvey, off Nevis, Feb. 18.
La Parfaite, fch. .	10	0	60	Roebuck, (S.S.) 24, A.S.Burrowes, off Martinique, Feb.19.
La Legere	13	0	130	Phaëton, 38, Hon.R.Stopford, and others, Channel, Feb.19.
La Coureur	24	0	150	Jafon, 38, C. Stirling, Channel ftation, Feb. 23.
(Name unkn.) fch. .	4	0	22	Cyane, 18, R. Manning, off St. Vincent's, Feb. 26.

Le

Names, Force in Guns, and Men.				By whom, where, and when, taken.
	Guns.	Swiv.	Men.	
Le Porc-Epic, lug. .	—	4	17	Refolution, (hired lugger,) 10, G. Broad, Downs ftation, Feb. 28.
La Revanche, lug. .	16	0	62	Marquis Cobourg, (hired cutter,) 16, Lieut. Webb, (funk,) North Sea, Feb.
L'Alexandrine, lug. .	1	4	28	Charon, (S.S.) 44, T. Manley, Channel, March 2.
Le Souffleur, cut. . .	4	2	40	Cameleon, (brig,) 18, R. R. Bowyer, Channel, March 2.
Le Lynx, (pierced for 13 guns) . .	10	0	70	King's Fifher, (floop,) 18, C. H. Pierrepont, Lifbon ftation, March 15.
Le Furet, fch. . . .	2	0	27	Hawke, (floop,) 16, E. Rotherham, off Grenada, Mar 15.
La Sophie, cutter .	4	0	20	Telemachus, (hired cutter,) 18, Lieut. Newton ; and Sea-Gull, (brig,) 18, H. Wray ; Channel, March 16.
L'Eugénie, brig . .	18	0	107	Magnanime, 44, Hon. M. De Courcy, March 16.
Auguftine, fch. . .	2	0	23	Solebay, 32, S. Povntz, off Antigua, March 17.
LaBonneCitoyenne, brig	12	0	65	Ruffel, 74, Sir H. Trollope ; and Jafon, 38, C. Stirling; in the Channel, March 20.
(Name unk.) cutter,	10	—	—	Echo, (floop,) 14, P. Halkett, deftroyed off Camperdown, March 23.
L'Emilie	18	0	110	Cleopatra, 32, I. Pellew, Channel ftation, March 26.
Le Céfar	16	0	80	Cambrian, 44, A. K. Legge, Channel ftation, March 27.
Le Vauteur, floop .	10	0	64	Matilda, 24, H. Mitford, northward of Antigua, March 29.
Le Pont de Lodi .	16	0	102	Cambrian, 44, Hon. A. K. Legge, Channel ftation, Mar.30.
Le Hardi, fchooner,	4	0	47	Lapwing, 28, T. Harvey, off St. Bartholomew, March 31.
L'Aigle, brig . . .	12	0	86	Matilda, 24, H. Mitford, northward of Antigua, March 31.
La Rofiere, fch. . .	2	0	15	La Concorde, 36, R. Barton, to windward of Montferrat, April 1.
L Audacieux	20	0	137	Magnanime, 44, Hon. M. De Courcy, April 2 (pierced for 22 guns).
La Violetta, floop .	6	0	36	Amphitrite, 28, C. Ekins, to windward of Barbadoes, April 3.
La Legere, brig . .	10	0	60	Nautilus, (floop,) 16, H. Gunter, and Narciffus, (hired cutter,) Lieutenant Wright, North Sea, April 4.
La Triumph, brig .	14	0	88	L'Aimable, 32, G. Lobb, and Scourge, (floop,) 22, S. Warren, off Porto Rico, April 6.
La Merveilleufe, fch.	6	0	39	Wright, (hired armed veffel,) 14, T Campbell, North Sea, April 7.
Le Sans Pareil, fch. .	1	8	21	Terrier, (hired bg,) 16, Lieut. Lowen, Downs, April 8
Le Chaffeur, fch. .	2	0	18	L'Aimable, 32, G. Lobb, and Scourge, (floop,) 22, S. Warren, off Porto Rico, April 8.
La Revanche, fch. (pierced for 12 g.)	10	0	54	Recovery, (fchooner,) 10, Lieutenant W. Rofs, Jamaica ftation, April 17.

    L'Efpiègle,

Names, Force in Guns, and Men.	Guns.	Swiv.	Men.
L'Efpiègle, fch. . .	2	0	18
La Renommée,⎫ fchooner . . ⎬	. 5	0	54
Le Brave, '(pierced⎫ for 22 guns) . .⎬	18	0	160
Jupiter, lugger . . .	8	0	36
(Name unknown,)⎫ fchooner . . . .⎬	4	0	35
L'Incrédule, fch. .	2	4	33
La Revanche, fch. .	12	0	88
Le Léopard	12	14	100
Le Sans Souci, lug. .	3	0	27
La Jeune Nantaife .	4	0	39
La Mutine, floop .	6	0	44
(Name unkn.) brig,	14	—	—
Bran le Bas, fch. .	8	0	82
Le Brutus, floop . .	6	0	51
Les Huits Amis . .	20	0	160
Sally	—	—	7
(Name unkn.) floop,	14	0	57
Goulette	—	—	11
Le Chaffeur, lugger,	4	0	48
La Vengeance,⎫ (pierced for 10 g.)⎬	6	0	71
La Zenodone, polac.	10	0	61
L'Annibale, brig .	14	0	97
L'Intrépide, floop .	10	0	58
La Mort, fchooner .	4	0	36
L'Aventure	—	—	14
Caroline	20	0	105
Le Brutus, lugger .	6	0	50

By whom, where, and when, taken.

L'Aimable, 32, G. Lobb, off Porto Rico, April 20.

Aftrea, 32, R. Dacres, on the Dogger-Bank, April 22.

Phœnix, 36, L. W. Halfted, fouth-weft of Cape Clear, April 24.

Cruifer, (floop,) 18, C. Wollafton, North Sea, April 27.

Refolution, 74, Halifax ftation, April 28.

Recovery, (fchooner,) 10, Licut. Rofs, Jamaica ftation, April 29.

Endymion, 44, Sir T. Williams, Irifh ftation, April 30.

Peterel, (floop,) 16, T. G. Caulfield, from St. Domingo to Lifbon, April 30.

Telemachus, (hired cutter,) 18, Lieutenant Newton, in the Channel, April 30.

Garland, (tender to the Prince of Wales, 98,) F. Banks, off Dominica, April.

Le Requin, (brig,) 12, Lieutenant W. W. Senhoufe, off St. Bartholomew's, May 1.

Scourge, (floop,) 22, S. Warren, deftroyed on St. Martin's, Weft Indies, May 1.

Tamer, 38, T. Weftern, to windward of Barbadoes, May 2.

La Victorieufe, 12, E. S. Dickfon, off Guadaloupe, May 7.

Endymion, 44, Sir T. Williams, Irifh ftation, May 10.

Ceres, 32, R. W. Otway, Jamaica ftation, May 12.

Rover, 18, G. Irvine, Halifax ftation, May 17.

Ceres, 32, R. W. Otway, Jamaica ftation, May 18.

Cruifer, (floop,) 18, C. Wollafton, North Sea, May 19.

Aftrea, 32, R. Dacres, Jamaica ftation, May 20.

Caroline, 36, W. Luke, near Cape Palos, Lifbon ftation, May 23.

Matilda, 24, H. Mitford, to windward of Antigua, May 29.

Lapwing, 28, T. Harvey, off St. Bartholomew's, May 29.

Charlotte, (fchooner,) 10, Lieutenant Williams, off Dominica, May 29.

Ceres, 32, R. W. Otway, Jamaica ftation, May 30.

Phœnix, 36, L. W. Halfted, latitude 49°, longitude 15° weft, May 31.

Endymion, 44, Sir T. Williams, Irifh ftation, May,
L'Hirondelle

Names, Force in Guns, and Men.	Guns.	Swiv.	Men.	By whom, where, and when, taken.
L'Hirondelle	10	—	—	Acaſta, 40, R. Lane, Jamaica ſtation, May.
(Name unknown) .	6	—	—	Ditto, May.
(Name unknown) .	6	0	40	Ditto, May *(pierced for 10 guns).*
St. Mary de Lou-⎰ vaine . . . . . . ⎱	2	0	25	Acaſta, 40, R. Lane, and Ceres, 32, R. W. Otway, Jamaica ſtation, May.
La Revanche	14	0	84	Thetis, 38, Hon. A. F. Cochrane, Halifax ſtation, May.
(Name unknown) .	6	—	—	Ditto, May.
La Legere, lugger .	4	0	35	Iris, 32, G. Briſac, off the Scaw, June 1.
La Mutinie, brig .	18	0	150	Ceres, 32, R. W. Otway, to windward of St. Juan, burnt, June 1.
Cargo, *(pierced for* ⎰ *4 guns)* . . . . ⎱	2	0	5	Ceres, 32, R. W. Otway, Jamaica ſtation, June 8.
L'Iſabelle, fchooner,	2	0	30	Lynx, (ſloop,) 16, R. Hall, coaſt of America, June 13.
Le Deſtin, fchooner,	4	0	46	Solebay, 32, S. Poyntz, off Martinique, June 13.
Four ſloops, &c. . .	—	—	—	Ceres, 32, R. W. Otway, Jamaica ſtation, fcuttled, June 20.
(Name unknown,)	20	—	—	Aurora, 28, H. Digby, coaſt of Spain, deſtroyed, June 22.
La Julie	18	0	120	Shannon, 32, A. Fraſer, latitude 50° north, longitude 21° weſt, June 23.
L'Etoile, ſloop . . .	6	0	53	Matilda, 24, H. Mitford, northward of Antigua, June 23.
Le Mentor, brig . .	14	0	79	Lynx, (ſloop,) 16, R. Hall, coaſt of America, June 27.
La Trompe	2	0	10	Acaſta, 40, R. Lane, Jamaica ſtation, June 30.
La Pouline, fch. . .	4	0	32	Regulus, 44, G. Eyre, Jamaica ſtation, July 7.
Le Mahomet, fch.	4	0	34	Hawke, (ſloop,) 16, E. Rotheram, off St. Lucia, July 8.
L'Heureux	16	0	112	Indefatigable, 44, Sir E. Pellew, off Bayonne, Auguſt 5.
La Vaillante	—	—	—	Indefatigable, 44, Sir E. Pellew, Weſtern ſtation, Auguſt 8.
Le Tigre, fettee . .	8	8	53	Naiad, 38, W. Pierrepont, 42 leagues weſt-north-weſt from Cape Finiſterre, Auguſt 11.
Invariable, fch. . .	4	0	20	Lapwing, 28, T. Harvey, Leeward-Iſland ſtation, Aug. 12.
La Colombe	12	0	64	Magnanime, 44, Hon. M. De Courcy, from Bayonne to the Weſt Indies, Auguſt 16.
Le Francois	2	6	23	El Corſo, (ſloop,) 18, B. James, Mediterranean, Aug. 24.
Le Mercure	18	0	132	Phaëton, Hon. R. Stopford, and Anſon, 44, P. C. Durham, near Bourdeaux, Auguſt 31.
Huffar, lug.	14	0	34	America, 64, J. Smith, North Sea, Auguſt.
Le Buonaparte, fch.	8	0	72	⎱ La Concorde, 36, R. Barton, and Lapwing, 28, T.
L'Amazone, fch. .	10	0	80	⎰ Harvey, Leeward-Iſles ſtation, between Auguſt 8 and
Le Sauveur, fch. .	4	0	20	September 8.
La Fortune, fch. .	2	0	22	
Le Dix Aout, bg .	12	0	50	Bittern, (ſloop,) 16, E. Kittoe, off Mariegalante, Weſt Indies, September 8.

G 3   L'Arraigné

Names, Force in Guns, and Men.	Guns.	Swiv.	Men.	By whom, where, and when, taken.
L'Arraigné, fch. ⎱ (pierced for 8 g.) ⎰	5	0	38	Triton, 32, J. Gore, from Cape Machicaco to Gulf St. Lawrence, September 28.
La Sophie	10	0	130	Endymion, 44, Sir T. Williams, Irifh Coaft, September.
Prefident Parker, cut.	12	0	50	Flora, 36, R. G. Middleton, and Caroline, 36, Lord H. Powlett, off Salvages, Lifbon ftation, October 4.
L'Intrépide, bg .	14	0	74	Matilda, 24, H. Mitford, off Antigua, October 5.
Le Levrier, bg . .	16	0	70	Phaëton, 38, Hon. R. Stopford, Channel ftation, Oct. 8.
(Name unkn.) row-b.	—	—	—	Deftroyed by the Pearl, 32, S. J. Ballard, under Dominica, October 10.
Le Scævola	10	0	73	Pearl, 32, S. J. Ballard, off Antigua, October 14.
L'Efpérance, lug. .	1	fw.	38	Boats of the Caroline, 36, Lord H. Powlett, deftroyed at Teneriffe ; October 16.
La Revanche . . .	—	—	—	Cambrian, 44, Hon..A. K. Legge, Channel, October 19.
Le Baret, polacre .	10	0	27	Caroline, 36, Lord H. Paulet ; and Flora, 36, R. G. Middleton ; off Teneriffe, October 20.
Le Vigilante . . .	14	0	50	Racoon, (brig,) 18, R. Lloyd, North Sea, (funk,) Oct. 20.
(Name unk.) lug. .	—	—	—	Driven on the rocks of Cape La Hogue, by the Arethufa, 38, T. Wolley, Oct. 21.
Le Tartar	—	—	—	Cormorant, 20, Lord M. R. Kerr, Mediterranean, Oct. 27.
L'Erin go Brah . .	10	8	45	Refolution, (hired cutter,) 10, Lieut. Broad ; and Plover, (floop,) 18, J. Chefhyre ; North Sea, Oct. 28.
(Name unkn.) fch.	4	0	30	Cut out of Port Nieu, Weft Indies, by the boats of the Queen, 98, and Lark, 16, J. Hayes,
L'Actif, brig . . .	8	0	36	Acafta, 40, R. Lane, Jamaica ftation,
(Name unkn.) fch.	6	0	60	Burnt by ditto, ditto,
La Triomphante, ⎱ fch. . . . . . . ⎰	6	0	66	Renommé, 44, R. Rolles, Jamaica ftation,
Laurette, fch. . . .	6	0	46	Surprife, 24, E. Hamilton, Jamaica ftation,
Bonaparte, fch. . .	6	0	50	Swallow, (floop) 18, W. Sanderfon, ditto,
La Belle en Cuiffe, ⎱ fchooner . . . . ⎰	4	0	57	Pelican, (brig,) 18, R. Philpot, ditto,
Petite Françaife, fch.	4	0	35	L'Amaranthe, 14, F. Vefey ; and Surprife, 24, E. Hamilton ; ditto,
La Guadaloupienne, ⎱ fch. . . . . . . ⎰	10	0	80	Amphitrite, 28, C. Ekins, Leeward-Ifland ftation,
La Prize de Matthe, fch.	8	0	65	Ditto　　　Ditto,
La Bourdelais, flp .	6	0	38	Ditto　　　Ditto,
La Profpérité, fch. .	8	0	61	Solebay, 32, S. Poyntz, ditto,
L'Indépendence, bg,	12	0	66	Pearl, 32, S. I. Ballard, ditto,

Between June, 1798, and Feb. 10, 1799.

Between Nov. 7 and Dec. 10.

Le

Names, Force in Guns, and Men.	Guns	Swiv.	Men.	By whom, where, and when, taken.
Le Quartorze Juil-let, brig .... }	14	0	65	Santa Margaritta, 36, G. Parker, ⎫ Between
La Jombie, cutter .	8	0	72	Leeward-Ifland ftation, ⎬ Nov. 7 &
(Name unkn.) fch.	12	—	—	Cyane, 18, R. Matfon, ditto, ⎭ Dec. 10.
				Deftroyed by Victorieufe, 12, E. S. Dickfon, Weft Indies, Nov. 10.
Succès	4	0	24	Lion, (hired cut.) Lt. Columbine, off Haftings, Nov. 13.
Le Tigre	—	—	—	Melpomene, 44, Sir C. Hamilton, Irifh ftation, Nov. 17.
L'Entreprife, lug. .	—	2	16	George, (hired cut.) Lt. C. Patey, off Alderney, Nov. 19.
L'Adolphe	6	0	42	El Corfo, (floop,) 18, Lt. Cor. Boger, Sts Gibr. Nov. 20.
La Réfolue, brig ..	18	0	70	Phaeton, 38, Hon. R. Stopford, Channel, Nov. 24.
(Name unkn.) . .	2	2	—	Corfo, (floop,) 18, Lieut. C. Boger, near Rofea-Bay, Dec.1.
(Name unkn.) . .	6	0	80	Victorieufe, 12, E. S. Dickfon; and Zephyr, 14, W. Champain; at Gurupano, Weft Indies, Dec. 4.
Le Serailleur, brig,	12	0	58	Caroline, 36, W. Bowen, Lifbon ftation, Dec. 4.
Le Calaifen, lug. .	4	0	18	Badger, (excife-cut.) T. R. Rudge, near Dungenefs, Dec.5.
La Reffource, brig,	10	0	66	Phaeton, 38, Hon. R. Stopford; and Stag, 32, J. S. Yorke; Channel ftation, Dec. 6.
La Cantabre, brig .	14	0	75	Cambrian, 44, Hon. A. K. Legge, in the Channel, Dec. 8.
L'Invincible Bona-parte ...... }	20	0	170	Boadicea, 38, R. G. Keats, Channel ftation, December 9.
La Rofée, brig ..	14	0	70	Triton, 32, E. Griffith, and St. Fiorenzo, 40, Sir H. B. Neale, bart. in the Channel, December.
(Name unkn.) cut.	—	—	—	A Spanifh fchooner, prize to the St. Fiorenzo, 40, under the command of a midfhipman, with-7 men, Dec.
L'Armée d'Italie,	18	0	117	La Perdrix, 24, A. C. Fahie, Weft Indies, December 12.
La Minerve	16	0	140	Indefatigable, 44, Sir E. Pellew, bart. 5 leagues fouth-weft from Ufhant, December 31.
L'Impromptu, brig,	14	0	64	Triton, 32, E. Griffith, on the paffage from Corunna to the Weftern Iflands, December 31.

1799.

Names, Force in Guns, and Men.	Guns	Swiv.	Men.	By whom, where, and when, taken.
La Rancune, cutter,	—	2	21	Pigmy, (cutter,) 14, Lieut. W. Shepheard, Channel, Jan. 8.
Le Bon Ordre, brig,	16	0	65	Clyde, 38, C. Cunningham, in the Channel, January 13.
Le Grand Indien .	20	0	125	Shannon, 32, A. Frafer, Irifh ftation, January 15.
Foudroyant, fhip. .	20	0	160	Phœnix, 36, L. W. Halfted, Irifh ftation, January 23.
L'Intrépide	20	0	160	Flora, 36, R. G. Middleton, Lifbon ftation, January 25.
(Name unkn.) cut.	16	—	—	Run down under the guns of the garrifon, in Guernfey, by Triton, 32, J. Gore, and captured there by the troops, January 29.
L'Aimable Victoire,	18	0	87	Triton, 32, J. Gore, between Alderney and the Start, Jan.30.

Le

Names, Force in Guns, and Men.	Guns.	Swiv.	Men.	By whom, where, and when, taken.
Le Boulonnois, cut.	14	0	70	Anfon, 44, P. C. Durham, and Ethalion, 38, G. Counteſs, Narth Sea, February 2.
La Gleneur, cutter .	6	0	32	Fly, (floop,) 16, Z Mudge, off Portland, February 6.
L'Eſcamoteur ...	3	0	34	Tranſfer, (floop,) 14, Lieut. G. Miller *(acting)*, Mediterranean, February 11.
La Prudente	18	0	100	Concorde, 36, R. Barton, Weſt Indies, Fcbruary 14.
L Aventure	14	0	130	Flora, 36, R. G. Middleton, Liſbon ftation, February 20.
Le Milan, cutter .	14	0	44	Boadicea, 38, R. G. Keats, and Atalante, (floop,) 16, A. J. Griffiths, in the Channel, February 20.
Le Jaſon, brig...	14	0	52	La Jaloufe, (brig,) 18, J. Temple, off the Texel, Feb. 23.
La Zelé	16	0	69	Melpomene, 44, Sir C. Hamilton, 9 leagues from the Saints, coaſt of Frınce, February 28.
(Name unknown) .	10	0	42	Rattler, (flp,) 16, J. M. Spread, Jamaica ftation,⎫ Between
(Name unkn.) fch.	10	0	79	Maidftone, 32, R. Donnelly, Jamaica ftation, ⎪ Feb. 12
(Name unkn.) fch.	8	—	—	Aquilon, 32, T. Boys, Jamaica ftation, ⎬ and
La Lione, fch....	5	0	60	Surprife, 24, E. Hamilton, Jamaica ftation, ⎪ April 15.
(Name unkn.) fch.	—	—	—	Lark, (flp,) 16, J W. Loring, Jamaica ftation,⎭
L Heureux Hazard,	16	0	94	Naiad, 38, W. Pierrepont, in the Bay of Biſcay, March 5 *(pierced for 20 guns)*.
L'Indéfatigable ...	18	0	120	Ethalion, 38, G. Counteſs, Channel ftation, March 6 *(pierced for 20 guns)*.
Le Requin, fhip ..	14	0	70	Boadicea, 38, R. G. Keats, Channel, but overſet the day after, by which a mafter's mate and ten men were loft, Mar. 8.
Le Mercure, fhip..	16	0	103	Melampus, 36, G. Moore, in the Bay of Biſcay, March.
Le Courier, fhip ..	16	—	—	The ſquadron of Commodore S. Hood, in the Mediterranean, March.
L'Hirondelle, brig .	—	24	67	Telegraph, (hired brig,) 16, Lieut. J. Worth, off the Iſle of Bas, March 18.
La Réſolue, brig ..	14	0	65	Spitfire, (floop,) 16, M. Seymour, 14 leagues north-north-weſt of Scilly, March 31.
L'Utile, brig	16	0	120	Boadicea, 38, R. G. Keats, in the Channel, April 1.
Argus, brig	18	0	130	Pomone, 44, R. C. Reynolds, off Cape Finifterre, April 3.
Le Coureur, lug. ..	4	6	46	Phœnix, (lugger privateer,) —— Hamon, 4 leagues ſouth-eaſt of St. Sebaftian, April 5.
(Name unknown) fh.	16	—	—	Driven on fhore and deftroyed by Majeftic, 74, G. Hope, and Transfer, (brig,) 14, G. Miller, Mediterranean, April 5.
Le Marfouin, lug. .	14	0	58	Aftrea, 32, R. Dacres, North Sea, April 10.
Le Vengeur, fch. ..	6	0	50	L'Amaranthe, (floop,) 10, F. Vefey, Jamaica ftation, April 13.
Le Papillon, brig ..	14	0	123	Melampus, 36, G. Moore, latitude 48° 30' north, longitude 15° weft, April 15.

Le

Names, Force in Guns, and Men.	Guns.	Swiv.	Men.	By whom, where, and when, taken.
Le Nautois, brig . . 14	14	o	150	Sunk by Melampus, 36, G. Moore, on being chafed by her in latitude 50° 20′ north longitude, 15° 20′ weft, and all the crew loft, April 18.
Le Vengeur, cutter, 14	14	o	105	Martin, 16, Hon. M. St. Clair, off the Scaw, in the North Sea, April 28.
La Legere 14	14	o	60	Flora, 36, R. G. Middleton, Lifbon ftation, April 28.
Ribôtteur, fch. . . . 6	6	o	26	Courier, (cutter,) Lieut. T. Searle, off the Texel, May 13.
La Rufe, lugger . . . 14	14	o	60	Kite, (brig,) 18, C. Lydiard, near the Scaw, North Sea, May 18.
Les Deux Freies . . 14	14	o	50	Cruizer, (brig,) 18, C. Wollafton, North Sea, May 21.
L'Aimable Thérefe, lugger 4	4	o	27	Ann, (hired cutter,) Lieut. R. Young, off Folkftone, May 25.
Le Vigie, fchooner . 14′	14′	o	71	Refolution, (cutter-privateer,) off Guernfey, W. Le Lachour, latitude 43° north, longitude 16° weft, May 25.
La Victoire, brig . . 16	16	o	160	La Révolutionnaire, 44, T. Twyfden, latitude 48° 30′ north, longitude 19° weft, May 30.
La Vénus, brig . . . 14	14	o	101	Indefatigable, 44, Hon. H. Curzon, in the Bay of Bifcay, May 31.
L'Hyppolite . . . . . —	—	—	—	La Révolutionnaire, 44, T. Twyfden, coaft of Ireland, June 2.
(Name unkn.) floop, 3	3	o	13	Cut out by the boats of the Regulus, 44, at Rio de la Hache, afterwards fcuttled, June.
Courageux 28	28	o	253	Alcmene, 32, H. Digby, near the Açores, or Weftern Iflands, June 21.
L'Hirondelle, lugger, 5	5	2	26	Hound, (brig,) 18, J. Wood, 8 leagues north-north-eaft from the Scaw, June 22.
Le Duquefne, brig . 16	16	o	129	Amphitrite, 28, C. Ekins, to windward of Antigua, June 26.
L'Anacréon, brig . . 16	16	o	125	Champion, 24, G. E. Hamond, North Sea, June 22.
Déterminé, fhip . . . 18	18	o	163	La Révolutionnaire, 44, T. Twyfden, off Ireland, June 29.
Le Courageux, lugger, 14	14	o	47	Cruizer, (brig,) 18, C. Wollafton, North Sea, July 13.
Rhuiter, brig 14	14	o	104	Flora, 36, R. H. Middleton, Lifbon ftation, July 25.
La Junon, fchooner. . 1	1	o	30	Trent, 36, R. W. Otway, Weft Indies, July.
Les Deux Amis, brig, 6	6	o	60	Alcmene, 32, H. Digby, Atlantic Ocean, Auguft 16.
Le Dragon, lugger . 16	16	—	—	Bufy, (floop,) 18, J. A. Ommanney, North Sea, Sept. 16.
L'Eclair, brig 10	10	4	83	Burnt by the Sceptre, 64, V. Edwards, Ifland of Rodriguez, in the Indian Ocean, September 19.
Le Bourdelais 26	26	o	220	} Révolutionnaire, 44, T Twyfden, and Phœbe, 36, R.
Le Grand Ferrailleur, 18	18	—	—	} Barlow, Irifh ftation, October.
L'Heureux 10	10	—	—	Stag, 32, J. S. Yorke, and Cambrian, 44, Hon. A. K. Legge, off Bourdeaux River, October 19.
				L'Hirondelle

Names, Force in Guns, and Men.	Guns.	Swiv.	Men.	By whom, where, and when, taken.
L'Hirondelle	14	6	50	Eurydice, 24, J. Talbot, and Snake, 16, J. Lewis, off Beachy-Head, November 10.
Le Petit Diable, cutt.	—	—	8	Ann, (hired cutter,) 12, Lieut. R. Young, off Beachy-Head, November 21.
(Name unkn.) lug. .	—	—	13	Fanny. (hired lugger,) 16, Lieut. W. Friffell, off the Start, November 21.
Le Guerrier, cutter .	14	o	44	Courier, (hired cutter,) 12, Lieut. T. Searle, North Sea, November 23.
Four Brothers, lug. .	4	o	44	Kent, (hired cutter,) 14, Lieut. W, Lanyon, off the North Foreland, November 26.
Républicain, lugger,	—	—	20	Camperdown, (hired cutter,) 14, Lieut. H. Wildey, near the South Foreland, Nov. 26.
Fantaifie, lugger ..	14	o	60	Jaloufe, (brig,) 18, J. Temple, in the North Sea, November 29.
Le Barras, fchooner .	14	o	57	Driver, (floop,) 16, J. Dunbar, in company with the Vigilant, (hired lugger,) off the Texel, November 30.
Le Vrai Décide, lug.	14	4	50	Racoon, (floop,) 18, R. Lloyd, in the Channel, Dec. 2.
L'Intrépide, lugger .	16	o	60	Ditto, ditto, December 3.
Le Succès, lugger ..	6	o	48	Atalante, (floop,) 16, A. J. Griffiths, Downs ftation, Dec. 4.
L'Heureufe Efpérance, lugger .. }	14	o	24	Speedwell, (hired fchooner,) Lieut. R. Tomlinfon, and Valiant, (hired lugger,) Lieut. Maxwell, in the Channel, December 5.
L'Heureux Spéculateur, brig .... }	14	o	58	Ditto, and Ditto, December 9.
L'Efpérance, lugger .	5	o	36	Netley, (fch.) 16, Lieut. F. G. Bond, Lifbon ftation, Dec. 22.
Le Furet	14	o	57	Viper, (cutter,) 12, Lieut. J. Pengelley, Channel, Dec. 26.
L'Aventurier, brig .	14	o	75	Amethyft, 38, J. Cooke, (1,) in the Channel, Dec. 29.
L'Aventure, fchooner,	14	o	42	Ariftocrat, (hired brig,) 18, Lieut. N. Wray, *(acting,)* in the Channel, December 30.

1800.

Names, Force in Guns, and Men.	Guns.	Swiv.	Men.	By whom, where, and when, taken.
Le Général Brune .	2	o	15	Cuftomhoufe-boat of Newhaven, and four other boats of volunteers, near Newhaven, January 6.
L'Avantageux ...	—	—	—	Ajax, 80, Hon. A. F. Cochrane, Channel ftation, Jan. 9.
Le Renard, lugger,	14	2	65	Nemefis, 28, T. Barker, in the Channel, January 12.
Le Modéré, lugger,	4	o	42	Nile, (3,) (hired lugger,) 10, S. Butcher, *(Mafter, acting,)* Downs ftation, Jan. 13.
La Vulture, fhip ..	22	o	137	Caroline, 36, W. Bowen, Lifbon ftation, Jan. 15.
Petite Victoire, fch.	2	o	52	La Legere, 24, Corn. Quinton, off Porto Rico, Jan. or Feb.

La

Names, Force in Guns, and Men.	Guns.	Swiv.	Men.	By whom, where, and when, taken.
La Victoire, fch. . .	10	0	60	Sunk under the batteries of Aquader, Weft Indies, by the Acafta, 40, E. Fellowes, January or February.
Le Courageux, lug. .	5	0	42	Suffifante, 14, J. Wittman, in company with the Havick, 18, P. Bartholomew, in the Channel, Jan. 29.
Le Grand Quinola } lug. car. &c.) . }	—	—	47	
La Vigoureufe, lug.	3	0	26	Camilla, 20, R. Larkan, coaft of France, Jan. 29.
Perféverance, fch. .	16	0	87	Unité, 38, J. P. Beresford, Leeward-Ifland ftation, Feb. 2
L'Egyptienne, lug.	15	0	66	Mercury, 28, T. Rogers, off the Ifle of Wight, Feb. 5.
L'Eole, brig . . .	10	0	80	Phœnix, 36, L. W. Halfted, in company with the Incendiary, (fire-fhip,) 14, R. D. Dunn, off Cape Spartel, Feb. 11.
Bougainville	18	0	82	Amazon, 38, E. Riou, Channel ftation, Feb. 14. (Loft, by running foul of the Amazon, on the night following; crew faved, excepting one.)
La Valliante, cutter,	14	0	130	Amethyft, 32, J. Cooke (1); and La Nymphe, 36, P. Frafer; in the Channel, Feb. 15.
Bellegarde, fhip . .	14	0	114	Phœbe, 36, R. Barlow, Irifh ftation, Feb. 21.
Vengeance	16	0	174	Néréide, 36, F. Watkins, Channel ftation, Feb. 28.
Le Furet, brig . . .	14	0	80	La Minerve, 42, G. Cockburn, Lifbon ftation, March 2.
Coureur, fhip	14	0	158	Révolutionnaire, 44, T. Twyfden, Irifh ftation, March 4.
Telegraph, brig . .	14	0	78	Kangaroo, (brig,) 18, E. Brace, Irifh ftation, March.
Le Maffena, lugger,	4	0	34	Plover, (floop,) 18, E. Galway, off Dunkirk, March 10.
L'Heureux, fhip . .	22	0	220	Phœbe, 36, R. Barlow, in the Channel, March 11.
Jofephina, cutter .	4	0	20	Suffifante, (floop,) 14, J. Wittman, in the Channel, Mar. 13.
(Name unknown,) } fchooner . . . . }	2	—	—	By the boats of the Lark, (floop,) 16, J. W. Lóring, Cuba, afterwards deftroyed, March 14.
Chafer, lugger . . .	14	0	37	Seaflower, (floop,) 16, Lieut. J. Murray, off Cape Frehel, March 19.
Le Perféverant, cut.	14	0	49	Cruifer, (brig,) 18, C. Wollafton, North Sea, March 23.
Confolateur, floop .	1	0	36	Surinam, 18, C. Cole, Leeward-Ifland ftation, March 24.
Plibuftier, brig . .	14	0	54	Cruizer, 18, C. Wollafton, North Sea, March 25.
La Cerberre, fchooner,	6	0	20	Uranie, 38, G. H. Towry, in the Channel, March 25.
Renard, floop . . .	3	0	15	Sûrinam, 18, C. Cole, Leeward-Ifland ftation, March 26.
La Penfée, fchooner,	4	0	65	Sans Pareil, 80, C. V. Penrofe, Leeward-Ifland ftation, March 27.
Sapaion, fchooner, .	6	0	48	
Victoire	2	0	28	Mutine, 14, W. Hofte, Mediterranean, March 29.
Le Mars, hip . . .	22	0	180	Amethyft, 38, J. Cooke, (1,) in the Channel, April 1
L'Inattenda, cutter .	2	0	25	Jaloufe, (brig,) 18, J. Temple, North Sea, April 5.
La Viginie, lugger,	14	0	53	Latona, 38, F. Sotheron, off Flamborough-Head, April 6.
				L'Innocente

Names, Force in Guns, and Men.	Guns.	Swiv.	Men	By whom, where, and when, taken.
L'Innocente	2	0	37	Gipfey, (tender,) Lieut. Tippett, Leeward-Ifland ftation, April 12.
L'Heureufe Société .	14	0	64	Spitfire, 16, M. Seymour, in the Channel, April 17.
Le Troifième, fch. .	14	0	68	⎫ Mayflower, (privateer,) of Guernfey, J. Le Bair, Bay of
Le Tarn	6	0	55	⎭ Bifcay, April.
L'Impregnable, cut.	14	—	—	Lark, (hired lugger,) 14, Lieut. J. H. Wilfon, on Vlie-Ifland, coaft of Holland. The crew, about 60, efcaped on fhore. April 24.
Rifque Tout	—	—	18	Daphne, 20, R. Matfon, Leeward-Ifland ftation, April 26.
La Mouche	20	0	145	La Minerve, 42, G. Cockburn, coaft of Spain, April.
Le Hardi, fch. . . .	18	0	194	Anfon, 44, P. C. Durham, Channel ftation, April 29.
Gen. Bernadotte, cut.	14	0	57	Arethufa, 38, T. Wolley, off Oporto, May 1.
Les Huits Freres, lug.	14	—	—	Lady Ann, (hired lugger,) 16, Lieut. J. Wright, off Flufhing, May 4.
L'Enfant Chérie de la Victoire . . . . . ⎱	1	2	22	Port Mahon, (brig,) 18, W. Buchanan, Mediterranean, May 8.
L'Intrépide	6	0	42	Speedy, (floop,) 14, Lord Vifcount Cochrane, Mediterranean, May 11.
L'Egyptienne, brig .	8	0	50	Incendiary, 14, R. D. Dunn, Mediterranean, May 12.
La Françoife, fch. .	12	0	42	La Loire, 46, J. Newman, on paffage to Lifbon, May 15.
La Vengeance, cut.	15	0	132	La Minerve, 42, G. Cockburn; and Netley, (ich.) 16, Lieut. F. G. Bond ; Mediterranean, May 15.
La Médie, fch. . . .	10	0	70	Diana, 38, A. Frafer, Leeward-Ifland ftation, May 17.
Le Scipio, fch. . . .	18	0	149	Endymion, 44, Sir T. Williams, on paffage to Mediterranean, May.
Le Rifque à Tout . .	2	0	16	Rofe, (2,) (hired cutter,) 8, Lieut. H. Richardfon, (1,) in company with the Dolphin, (hired cutter,) off Cape Barfleur, May 31.
Gen. Maffena, fch. .	16	0	150	Tamer, 38, T. Weftern, Leeward-Ifland ftation, June 1.
La Volante, fch. . .	1	0	10	Gipfey, (tender,) Lieut. Tippett, Leeward-Ifland ftation, June 7.
L'Hirondelle, fch. .	—	4	6	Southampton, 32, J. Harvey, Leeward-Ifland ftation, June 9.
L'Augufte, lett. marq.	10	0	50	Melpomene, 44, Sir C. Hamilton, coaft of France, June 17.
Le Vengeur, brig . .	14	0	120	Indefatigable, 44, Hon. H. Curzon, Channel ftation, June.
A row-boat	—	—	19	Quebec, 32, H. W. Bayntun, Jamaica ftation, ——.
Deux Amis, cutter .	—	—	8	Conftance, (hired brig,) 12, Lieut. M. Wright, off St. Aldan's Head, June 19.
L'HeureuxCourier, bg,	14	0	54	Spitfire, 16, M. Seymour, Channel ftation, June 19.

Fidelle,

Names, Force in Guns, and Men.	Guns	Swiv.	Men.	By whom, where, and when, taken.
Fidelle, fch.	4	o	61	Gipfey and Pickle, (tenders,) Leeward-Ifland ftation, June 30.
L'Induftrie, fch . . .	6	o	23	Diana, 38, A. Frafer, Leeward-Ifland ftation, July 13.
Jupiter, tartan . . .	—	—	—	Conftance, 24, J. B. Hay, Mediterranean, July 13.
La Fortune, fch. . .	22	o	188	Ruby, 64, S. Ferris, on the paffage from St. Helena, July 14.
La Gironde	16	o	141	Fifgard, 44, T. B. Martin, in the Channel, July.
Conftitution, tartan,	—	—	—	Speedy, (floop,). 14, Lord Vifcount Cochrane, Mediterranean, July 19.
La Revanche, fch. .	14	o	80	Uranie, 44, G. H. Towry, near Cape Ortegal; July 28.
Providence, felucca,	2	o	23	Cameleon, (brig,) 18, F. L. Maitland, ·Mediterranean, Auguft 4.
L'Alerte	14	o	84	Fifgard, 44, T. B. Martin, in the Channel, ——.
Ajax, lugger	4	o	23	Hazard, (cutter-privateer,) J. Hocquard, off Guernfey, Aug. 4.
Trompeur, cutter .	—	—	—	Fly, (floop,) 16, Z. Mudge, in the Channel, Auguft 24.
La Guepe, fhip, (burthen 300 tons, and pierced for 22 guns)	18	o	161	By the boats of Rear Admiral Sir John Borlafe Warren's fquadron, under the command of Lieut. H. Burke, of the Renown, clofe to the batteries in Vigo-Bay, Auguft 29. The enemy had 25 men·killed, and 40 wounded. The Britifh 4 killed and 23 wounded, including Lieut. Burke, among the latter.
Général Holtz . . .	2	o	26	Termagant, 18, W. Skipfey, Mediterranean, Sept. 4.
Petit Chaffeur, cut.	1	—	—	Weazle, (floop,) 16, W. Durban, off Portland, September 19.
(Name unkn.) floop,	—	—	—	Néréide, 36, F. Watkins, at the furrender of Curacoa, September 23.
Gen. Touffaint, fch.	4	o	70	Alarm, 32, R. Rolles, off St. Domingo, ——.
Le Diable à Quatre, fch, ...	16	o	150	Thames, 32, W. Lukin, in company with L'Immortalite, 36, H. Hotham, Bay of Bifcay, Oct. 26.
Renard, cutter . . .	2	o	13	Nile, (3,) (hired lugger,) 14, S. Butcher, (Mafter, acting,) off Folkftone, Nov. 1.
L'Actif, brig . . ; .	16	o	137	Thames, 32, W. Lukin, Bay of Bifcay, Nov. 30.
L'Eclair, cutter . . .	3	o	20	Lord Duncan, (hired cutter,) 12, Lieut. W. Wells, off Shoreham, Dec. 13.

DUTCH

DUTCH PRIVATEERS TAKEN OR DESTROYED.

1796.

Names, Force in Guns, and Men				By whom, where, and when, taken.
	Guns.	Swiv.	Men.	
(Name unkn.) cut.	12	—	—	Admiral Duncan's fquadron, coaft of Norway, April.

1797.

	Guns.	Swiv.	Men.	
Stuiver	10	0	48	Aftrea, 32, R. Dacres, off the Scaw, June 1.
Brutal, lug.	6	0	32	Nautillus, (floop,) 16, H. Gunter, and Fox, (cutter,) off Fleckery, in Norway, June 12.
De Klyne Sperver .	6	0	28	Nautilus, (floop,) 16, H. Gunter, and others, off the Scaw, July 2.
Le Batave	12	0	54	Roebuck, (S.S.) A. S. Burrowes, off Barbadoes, July 6.
Unity, fch.	10	0	50	Proferpine, 28, W. T. Lake, fouthward of Shetland, Auguft 3.
Goede Verwayteng, floop	8	0	28	Swan, (floop,) 14, H. Carew, North Sea, Auguft 12.
De Brave, fch. . . .	5	8	25	Albatrofs, (floop,) 18, G. Scott, 28 leagues S. W. Naze of Norway, Sept. 8.
D'Ondelboarlaid, fch.	10	0	46	L'Efpiègle, (floop,) 16, J. Boorder, off the coaft of Holland, September 23.

1798.

	Guns.	Swiv.	Men.	
Courier	—	—	—	Scorpion, (floop,) 16, J. T. Rodd, North Sea, April.
Sea-Hound, lug. . .	7	4	30	Hound, (floop,) 18, J. Wood, 10 leagues from the Scaw, June 14.
De Efle Andene-ming, fch. . . .	8	0	38	Charlotte, (fchooner,) 10, Lieut. Williams, off Demerary river, July 9.
Proferpine, fch. . .	2	0	13	Deftroyed by La Victorieufe, 12, E. S. Dickfon, in company with the Zephyr, 14, W. Champain, near Cape Three Points, Weft Indies, Dec. 2.

1799.

	Guns.	Swiv.	Men.	
Flufhinger	4	0	28	Marfhal de Cobourg, (hired brig,) Lieut. T. O'Neil, off the Texel, Feb. 1.
Pegafus	—	—	—	Iris, 32, G. Brifac; and Jane, (hired lugger,) 14, Lieut. Tait; North Sea, Sept. 15.

SPANISH

SPANISH PRIVATEERS TAKEN OR DESTROYED.

1797.

Names, Force in Guns, and Men.	Guns.	Swiv.	Men.	By whom, where, and when, taken.
(Name unkn.).lug.	1	0	38	King's Fiſher, (ſloop,) 18, E. Marſh, coaſt of Spain, January 23.
(Name unkn.) ſch.	12	0	60	Ditto, run on ſhore, ditto.
St. Chriſtopher, bg,	18	0	120	Lapwing, 28, R. Barton, northward of Bermuda, Feb. 15.
El Atrebedo, alias La Conception,	—	—	—	St. Albans, 64, W. Lechmere, Feb. 28.
(Name unkn.) cut.	6	—	—	Magicienne, 32, W. H. Rickets, Jamaica ſtation, Feb.
La Nativeta,let.of m.	16	0	50	Diligence, (brig,) 16, R. Mends, Weſt Indies, March 3.
Piteous Virgin Maria, brig . . .	10	8	42	Viper, (cutter,) 12, Lieut. Pengelly, Straits of Gibraltar, March 13.
El Principe de Paz,bg,	20	0	100	Boſton, 32, J. N. Morris, near Vigo, June 4.
St.Barnardo, aliasEl Conqueſtador . .	12	0	75	Ditto, coaſt of Portugal, June 16.
San Francisco, alias Los Amigos, bg,	14	0	53	Santa Margaritta, 36, G. Parker, Iriſh Coaſt, June 21.
(Name unknown,) xebeque	—	—	—	Hamadryad, 36, T. Elphinſtone, Straits of Gibral. June 30.
St. Joſe y Nueſtra Senora de Begoyna,	16	0	52	Pallas, 32, Hon. H. Curzon, lat. 44° N. long. 15° W. July 16.
El Domini Lucas, lug.	2	12	28	Speedy, (ſloop,) 14, H. Downman, 20 leagues, S.W. of Oporto, Auguſt 1.
El Derrepente, lug. .	4 fw.		85	Doris, 36, Lord Ranelagh, Iriſh ſtation, Auguſt 26.
Palma, ſch.	2	4	28	Speedy, (ſloop,) 14, H. Downman, off Ville de Condé, Liſbon ſtation, September 13.
San Noberta, ſch. .	4 fw.		42	Cerberus, 32, J. Drew, Iriſh ſtation, Sept.
(Name unknown,) Spaniſh packet .	6	—	—	Diligence, (brig) 16, R. Mends, La Renommée, 44, R. Rolles, and Hermione, 32,H.Pigot,Jamaica ſtation,Sept.
Pilgrim, lug.	3	0	22	Speedy, (ſloop,) 14, H.Downman, Liſbon ſtation, Dec. 21.
(Name un.)g.-b. lge,	—	—	—	Deſtroyed near the Havannah, Dec.

1798.

La Oliva, ſch. . .	4	12	40	Speedy, (ſloop,) 14, H. Downman, Liſbon ſtation, Jan. 1.
La Caſualided, ſch.	6	0	17	Aurora, 28, H. Digby, weſtward of Cape Finiſterre, Jan. 17.

San

Names, Force in Guns, and Men.	Guns	Swiv.	Men.	By whom, where, and when, taken.	
San Jofef, fch. . .	6	10	40	Thalia, 36, Lord H. Paulet, Feb. 27.	
Victoria, brig . . .	14	10	—	Ditto, March 4.	
St. Jofe, alias El Gavelan, lug. . .	6	0	44	Speedy, (floop,) 14, H. Downman, Lifbon ftation, Mar. 15.	
Union, let. of marq.	12	0	32	Indifpenfable, (let. marq.) 35 lea. S.W. of Cape Horn, Mar.	
L'Amiable Juana .	6	0	46	Hind, 28, J. Larcom, Halifax ftation, April 22.	
St. Mary	4	0	28	Acafta, 40, R. Lane, Jamaica ftation, May 1.	
St. Antonio	—	—	—	Ditto, May 12 *(pierced for 14 guns)*.	
L'Avantivia Ferolina, lug.	1	4	26	King's Fifher, (floop,) 18, C. H. Pierrepont, off Vigo, May 26.	
St. Jofef de Victoire,	8	0	50	Acafta, 40, R. Lane, 6 lea. to windward of St. Juan, burnt, July 2 *(pierced for 16 guns)*.	
St. Michael Acandoa,	6	0	28	Acafta, 40, R. Lane, Jamaica ftation, July 13.	
Lorenzo el Diligenti	—	—	—	King's Fifher, 18, E. Marfh, Lifbon ftation,	Between June, 1798, and Feb. 10, 1799.
L'Aimable Marfeilles, fch. floop,	4	0	40	Queen, 98, V. Ad. Parker, Captain Dobfon, Jamaica ftation,	
Cincinnatus, arm. fch.	2	0	33	Acafta, 40, R. Lane, Ditto,	
Penada, armed fhip .	14	0	40	Trent, 36, R. W. Otway, and Squirrel, 24, J. Hamftead, Ditto,	
Neptune, brig	4	0	23	Renommé, 44, R. Rolles, and Squirrel, 24, J. Hamftead, Ditto,	
Julie, fchooner . . .	4	0	12	Magicienne, 32, W. Ogilvy, Ditto,	
(Name unkn.) fch. .	6	—	—	St. Fiorenzo, 40, Sir H. B. Neale, bart. Channel ftation, December.	

1799.

La Prudencia, fch. .	1	8	34	Endymion, 44, Sir T. Williams, on paffage from Lifbon to England, January.
La Canfalidad . . .	6	8	40	
N. S. del Pont St. Bonaventa	8	0	55	Fairy, (floop,) 16, J. S. Horton, Channel ftation, January 11.
La Vierga de Rofario	14	0	90	Centaur, 74, J. Markham, Mediterranean, February 2.
(Name unknown) .	1	2	0	Lark, 16, J. W. Loring, Jamaica ftation, February.
N. S. del Carmen, *alias* Diligente, lg	2	0	21	Flora, 36, R. G. Middleton, Lifbon ftation, February 27.
Santo Chrifto del Gracia, am. vef.	8	—	—	Speedy, 14, J. Brenton, and Defender, (privateers,) of Gibraltar, off Cape de Gatt, Mediterranean, Auguft 9.
(Name unkn.) ditto,	10	—	—	
(Name unkn.) ditto,	4	—	—	

(Names

Names, Force in Guns, and Men.	Guns.	Swiv.	Men.	By whom, where, and when, taken.
(Names unkn.) 2 lg.	—	—	—	Netley, (fch.) 16, Lieut F. G. Bond, Lifbon ftation, Nov. 1.
El Orely, y los Tres Amigos, fch. . .	4	4	52	Ditto, Bay of Bifcay, November 14.
Afturiana, let. mar.	24	0	180	Amphion, 32, R. H. A. Baker, in company with the Alarm, 32, R. Rolles, Jamaica ftation, Nov. 25.
Felicidad, lug. . . .	5	0	36	Netley, (fch.) 16, Lieut. F. G. Bond, Lifbon ftation, Dec. 24.
St. Antonio y Animas, *alias* Aurora, fchooner .	6	0	46	Ditto, December 25.
Sta Levirata y Animas	2	0	38	Caftor, 32, E. L. Gower, off Oporto, December 25.

1800.

Names, Force in Guns, and Men.	Guns.	Swiv.	Men.	By whom, where, and when, taken.
Brilliant	8	0	63	Deftroyed by the Revenge, (privateer,) R. Hofier, off the coaft of Spain, January 4.
N. S. del Carmen, lug.	2	0	44	Maria, (privateer,) J. Doyle, in latitude 42° 10′ north longitude, 9° 15′ weft, January 24.
Aquilla, *(pierced for 22 guns)*	4	—	—	Apollo, 36, P. Halkett, latitude 43° 9′ north, longitude 12° weft, February 11.
El Batador, brig . . .	14	0	83	Cormorant, 20, Hon. C. Boyle, in latitude 45° 45′ north, longitude 10° 29′ weft. February 24.
La Louife, fchooner .	8	0	55	Stork, 18, W. Parker, Jamaica ftation, March.
(Name unkn.) fch. letter of mar. .	16	—	—	Trent, 36, R. W. Otway, Ditto, Ditto.
St. Pedro Apoftle, *alias* El Efcariotte, lugger . . .	5	0	37	Netley, (fchooner,) 16, Lieut. F. G. Bond, Mediterranean, March 17.
Corunefa, fhip . . .	16	0	90	Flora, 36, R. G. Middleton, off the coaft of Portugal, March 20.
St. Antonio y Animas, *alias* Aurora, fchooner . . .	10	0	55	Flora, 36, R. G. Middleton, Lifbon ftation, April 9.
Nueftra Senora del Carmo	1	0	34	La Minerve, 42, G. Cockburn, coaft of Spain, April.
San Jofef, lugger . .	4	0	38	Endymion, 44, Sir T. Williams, on paffage to the Mediterranean, May.
El Intripido, lugger .	2	0	21	
La Animas el Sola, *alias* Defcuite, lug.	—	—	—	Netley, (fchooner,) 16, Lieut. F. G. Bond, Mediterranean, May 16.

El

Names, Force in Guns, and Men.	Guns	Swiv.	Men,	By whom, where, and when, taken.
El Severo	—	10	26	} Anſon, 44, P. C. Durham, and Conſtance, 24, J. B. { Hay, Mediterranean, June 29.
Gibraltar	4	0	50	
La Virgin del Car-} men, xebec ... }	2	8	31	Jolly-boat of the Thalia, 36, J. Niſbet, commanded by Lieutenant G. D. Porter, Mediterranean, July 29.
(Name unkn.) feluc.	1	0	35	Melampus, 36, G. Moore, Jamaica ſtation, between May and Auguſt.
La Confiance, feluc.	3	0	55	Alarm, 32, R. Rolles, Weſt Indies.
N. S. del Carmen la} Confianza .... }	2	0	26	Netley, (ſchooner,) 16, Lieut. F. G. Bond, coaſt of Portugal, September 28.
Atalante, cutter ..	10	0	56	Hawke, (privateer,) T. Alti, coaſt of Portugal, Oct. 21.
San Miguel, alias } Alertta, ſchooner, }	9	0	65	Netley, (ſchooner,) 16, Lieut. F. G. Bond, coaſt of Portugal, November 7.
St. Jago, ſchooner .	10	0	60	Brilliant, 28, Hon. C. Paget, Channel ſtation, Nov. 18.
San Joſef, alias Lar-} con ...... }	6	0	40	Concorde, 36, R. Earton, off Oporto, December.

COLONIES, SETTLEMENTS, &c.

Taken from the Enemy, in which the Navy have been concerned, from the Commencement of Hoſtilities in 1793.

THE ISLAND OF TOBAGO, in the Weſt Indies, *F.*; taken April 15, 1793, by the land-forces, under Major-General Cuyler, with the Truſty, 50, Vice-Adm. Sir J. Laforey, bart. Capt. J. Drew; and Nautilus, 16, Hon. H. Powlett.

THE ISLANDS OF ST. PIERRE AND MIQUELON, near Newfoundland, *F*; ſurrendered May 14, 1793, to the land-forces under Brigadier-General Ogilvie, in conjunction with the Aligator, 28, W. Affleck.

PONDICHERRY, the laſt of the French ſettlements in India which ſurrendered to the Britiſh arms, capitulated to the land-forces under Colonel Braithwaite, Auguſt 23, 1793, the port having been previoufly blockaded by the Minerva, 38, Rear-Admiral the Hon. W. Cornwallis, Capt. J. Whitby ; and three Indiamen.

TOULON: taken poffeffion of Auguft 28, 1793, in confequence of propofitions made by the inhabitants to Vice-Adm. Lord Hood. The forts which refifted were taken by the Britifh under protection of the Meleager, 32, C. Tyler ; and Tartar, 28, T. F. Freemantle ; fupported by the Egmont, 74, A. Dickfon ; Robuft, 74, Hon. G. K. Elphinftone; Courageux, 74, Hon. W Waldegrave; and Coloffus, 74, C. M. Pole. Being no longer tenable, it was evacuated Dec. 18, when many of the French fhips, &c. which could not be gotten away, were deftroyed. *See French fhips loft, &c.*

THE WESTERN, or FRENCH, PART of ST. DOMINGO. LA GRAND ANCE, including the quarter at Jeremie, taken poffeffion of Sept. 20, 1793, in confequence of a voluntary capitulation made by the Council of Public Safety of that part of the ifland, by the Europa, 50, Com. J. Ford, Capt. G. Gregory ; accompanied by the Gœlan, 14, T. Welley, and FlyingFifh, (fchooner,) Lieut. Prevoft. The Commodore remained here but a few hours, when he failed for CAPE ST. NICOLAS MOLE, which furrendered on fimilar terms, Sept. 22. The parifhes of *St. Marc* and *Gonaives* furrendered to Major Grant, Commandant at St. NicolasMole, in Dec. 1793 ; and the parifhes of *Leogane, Arcahaye,* and *Jean de Rabel,* with *Mircbalais,* near Port-au-Prince, furrendered in Jan. 1794, on the fame conditions. At this time. Commodore Ford blockaded Port-au-Prince, and fuffered no veffels to enter. On the 3d of February, 1794, CAPE TIBERON was attacked, and taken, by the forces under Lieut.-Col. Whitelock, on the 23d of that month : the poft of *L'Acul,* at the extremity of the plain of Leogane, was taken, by ftorm, by the fame forces ; and, on the 4th of June fucceeding, PORT-AU-PRINCE was taken by the land-forces, under Brig.-Gen. Whyte, fupported by Commodore Ford's fquadron. The fhips entitled to fhare in the prize, arifing from this capture, were as follows : viz. Europa, 50, Com. J. Ford, Capt. G. Gregory ; Sceptre, 64, J. R. Dacres ; Irrefiftible, 74, J. Henry ; Belliqueux, 64, J. Brine ; Hermione, 32, J. Hills ; Iphigenia, 32, P. Sinclair ; Magicienne, 32, G. Martin ; Penelope, 32, B. S. Rowley ; Succefs, 32, F. Roberts ; Alligator, 28, T. Surridge ; L'Actif, 16, ———— ; Fly, (floop,) 16, T. Affleck ; Jack Tar, (floop,) 16, ———— ; Swan, (floop,) 14, H. Pigot ; Marie Antoinette, 10, Lt. J. Parkins ; Flying-Fifh, (fchooner,) Lieut. Prevoft ; and Mofquito, (g.-v.) ————. The town and poft of Leogane fell again into the power of the French, aided by a numerous corps of revolted negroes, Oct. 21, 1794. The garrifon of Cape Tiberon was evacuated by the Britifh, in confequence of powerful attacks on the part of the enemy, Dec. 24, following. And finally, on the 30th of April, 1798, Port-au-Prince, St. Marc's, &c. with their dependencies, were evacuated by the Britifh forces, under Brigadier-General the Hon. T. Maitland, on the French General Touffaint L'Ouverture engaging, in the moft folemn manner, to guarantee the lives and properties of the inhabitants.

LEEWARD ISLANDS. The armament for an expedition againft the French Weft India iflands, failed from England, Nov. 26, 1793. Its fuccefs from the nature of the fervice was dependent on the joint operations of Navy and Army : The former was therefore entrufted to the able direction of Vice-Admiral Sir John Jervis, K. B. ; and the latter to General Sir

Charles

Charles Grey, K. B. The event juſtified the confidence of their country; for never was ſucceſs more rapid, nor ever obtained by greater diſplay of individual and perſonal enterpriſe. The
ſucceſſive objects of attack were, Martinico, St. Lucia, Les Iſles des Saints, Mariegalante, and
Defeada: they were all accompliſhed between the 2d of February, 1794, and April 20, following; a ſhort period of about eleven weeks. MARTINICO was ſurrendered on very honourable conditions, by General Rochambeau, March 22, after a brave reſiſtance; during which,
the Britiſh had 89 killed, and 236 wounded, including among the former, Capt. J. Milne, of
the Avenger (ſloop), and among the latter, Capt. S. Tatham, of the Dromedary. The conqueſt of St. Lucia was achieved, on the 3d of April, without the loſs of one Britiſh ſoldier or
ſeaman. The SAINTS were taken poſſeſſion of, without any loſs, on the 10th of April.
That part of the ISLAND of GUADALOUPE, called *Grande Terre*, was taken by ſtorm, in the
morning of the 12th; and that part called *Baſſe Terre*, with its dependencies, namely Mariegalante, Defeada, &c. ſurrendered, on the ſame honourable terms as were granted to Martinico
and St. Lucia, April 20. In the operations againſt Guadaloupe, the Britiſh had 17 killed and
62 wounded.

The following are the names of the ſhips which compoſed the naval force under Vice-
Admiral Sir J. Jervis, and which ſhared in theſe conqueſts: viz. Aſia, 64, J. Brown; Aſſu-
rance, 44, V. C. Berkley; *(St. Lucia and Guadaloupe.)* Avenger, (ſloop,) 16. J. Milne *;
Boyne, 98, Vice-Admiral Sir J. Jervis, Capt. Geo. Grey; Beaulieu, 40, J. Saliſbury †;
Blanche, 32, C. Parker ‡; Blonde, 32, J. Markham, *(Martinico only;)* Bulldog, (ſloop,) 14,
E. Browne, *(Guadaloupe only:)* Ceres, 32, R. Incledon; Dromedary, (S.S.) 24, S. Tatham;
Experiment, 44, S. Miller; Irreſiſtible, 74, J. Henry; Inſpector, (ſloop,) 16, W. Bryer;
Nautilus, (ſloop,) 16, J. Carpenter; Quebec, 32, J. Rogers; Roebuck, 44, A. Chriſtie;
Rattleſnake, (ſloop,) 16, M. H. Scott, *(Martinico and St Lucia;)* Roſe, 28, E. Riou §; Re-
tort, Hon. C. Herbert, *(St. Lucia and Guad.;)* Santa Margaritta, 36, E. Harvey; Solebay,
32, W. H. Kelly; Seaflower, (cutter,) 14, W. Pierrepont; Terpſichore, 32, S. Edwards;
Ulyſſes, 44, R. Morice; Undaunted, 32, J. Carpenter; Vengeance, 74, Commodore C.
Thompſon, Capt. Hon. H. Powlett; Veteran, 64, C. E. Nugent; Veſuvius, (bomb,) 8. C.
Sawyer; Winchelſea, 32, Lord Viſcount Garlies; Woolwich, 44, J. Parker; Zebra, (ſloop,)
16, R. Faulknor ‖; Tickler, (gun-boat,) Henry Raye; Venom, (gun-boat,) T. H. Wilſon;
Teaſer, (gun-boat,) J. Hope; Vexer, (gun-boat,) R. Smith; Spiteful, (gun-boat,) J. H.
Sparkes; and Tormentor, (gun-boat,) Lieut W. Wells.

In the reduction of theſe iſlands, Major-General His Royal Highneſs Prince Edward, acting
under the orders of General Sir Charles Grey, was particularly diſtinguiſhed by the active and
gallant part which he executed in different engagements.

---

* Succeeded by H. W. Bayntun.   § Succeeded by M. H. Scott.
† ————— E. Riou.   ‖ ————— R. Bowen.
‡ ————— R. Faulknor.

CAPTURED FROM THE ENEMY.   81

In the beginning of June, 1794, a fuperior French force, which had failed from Rochfort in the month of April, regained poffeffion of Guadaloupe ; the Britifh forces, then in that ifland, being inadequate to its retention. St. Lucia was for the fame reafon evacuated June 19, 1795. The latter ifland, with its dependencies, was however retaken May 25, 1796, by the combined force, under Lieutenant-General Sir Ralph Abercrombie, K. B. and Rear-Admiral Sir H. C. Chriftian, K. B. whofe fquadron confifted of the Thunderer, 74, Sir H. C. Chriftian, Capt. James Bowen ; Alfred, 74, T. Drury ; Ganges, 74, R. M'Doual ; Vanguard, 74, S. Miller ; Vengeance, 74, T. M. Ruffell ; Minotaur, 74, T. Louis ; Invincible, 74, W. Cayley ; Grampus, 54, J. Williamfon ; Malabar, 54, T. Parr ; Madras, 54, J. Dilkes ; Arethufa, 38, T. Wolley ; Aftrea, 32, R. Lane ; L'Aimable, 32, C. S. Davers ; Ariadne, 20, H. L. Ball ; Beaulieu, 40, L. Skynner ; Charon, 44, J. Stevenfon ; Hebe, 38, M. H. Scott ; Laurel, 20, R. Rolles ; Matilda, 24, H. Mitford ; La Prompte, 30, G. Eyre ; Tourterelle, 30, E. Fellowes ; Undaunted, 40, H. Roberts ; Albicore, 16, R. Winthorp ; Beaver, 18, S. G. Warner ; Fury, 16, H. Evans ; Bull-dog, 14, G. F. Ryves ; Lacedemonian, (brig,) 16, ——; Pelican, 16, J. C. Searle ; Roebuck, 24, A. S. Burrowes ; Thorn, 16, Lieut. J. Hamftead ; Terror, (bomb,) 8, Hon. D. Douglas ; Victorieufe, 12, J. Mainwaring ; Requin, 12, Lieut. W. Champain ; the Frederic, Charlotte, and Berbice, (armed ftore-fhips,) and Queen Charlotte, (cutter.)

CORSICA. The Britifh fleet on the 24th of January, 1794, fet fail from its rendezvous in the Bay of Hieres, having for the object of its expedition to diflodge the enemy from Baftia, St. Fiorenzo, and Calvln, in the Ifland of Corfica. An attack was firft made upon ST. FIORENZO and the pofts which defended it, with a view to gain the undifturbed poffeffion of the Gulf of St. Fiorenzo, for the Britifh navy in the Mediterranean. The military force deftined for this purpofe was commanded by Lt.-Gen. David Dundas, and Adm. Lord Hood was commander-in-chief of the fleet. The town of St. Fiorenzo was evacuated by the enemy on the 19th of February, the ftrong pofts on the weftern fide of the Gulf having been previoufly taken ; but not without repeated attacks and the moft arduous perfeverance. The town and citadel of BASTIA, with the feveral forts upon the heights, furrendered May 22, 1794, upon an honourable capitulation to the Britifh forces, after having been befieged from the 4th of April. CALVI furrendered upon fimilar conditions, Auguft 10, 1794, after a fiege of 51 days. It was here that the brave Capt. W. Serocold was killed by a grape-fhot.

The Republican forces were by this event driven out of Corfica. The Britifh retained poffeffion until October, 1797, when the enemy having fucceeded in eftablifhing very powerful reinforcements, the ifland was found untenable, and evacuated.

The fhips which fhared in the reduction of this Ifland were as follows. ST. FIORENZO : — Alcide, 74, Comm. R. Linzee, Capt. J. Woodley ; Aurora, ——— ; Captain, 74, S. Reeve ; Egmont, 74, A. Dickfon ; Fortitude, 74, W. Young, B*; L'Impérieufe, 40, W. Wolfcley,

* The letters B & C denote Baftia and Calvi ; the fhips, to whofe names they are affixed, fhared alfo in the reduction of thofe places.

B & C;

B & C; Le Jean Bart, (gun-boat,) B & C ; Juno, 32, S. Hood; Meleager, 32, C. Tyler; Princeſs Royal, 98, R.-Adm. S. G. Goodall, Capt. J. C. Purvis, B ; Romulus, 36, J. Sutton ; Roſe, (cut.) B ; St. George, 98, R -Adm. Gell, Capt. T. Foley ; and Victory, 100, Adm. Lord Hood, Capt. J. N. Inglefield, and Capt. J. Knight, B & C. — BASTIA : — Agamemnon, 74, H. Nelſon ; Cyclops, 28, D. Gould ; L'Eclair, 20, G. H. Towry ; Fox, (cut.) C ; Gorgon, 44, J. Wallis ; Illuſtrious, 74, T. L. Frederick ; Modeſte, 40, T. B. Martin ; Nemeſis, 28, S. H. Linzee ; Proſelyte, 24, ——— ; Sincere, 18, ———, C ; and Swallow, (cut.) C. —CAL- vi : — L'Aigle, 36, S. Hood ; L'Aimable, 32, Sir H. Burrard, bart. ; Dido, 28, Sir C. Hamil- ton, bart. ; Dolphin, (hired ſloop,) 44, Lt. R. Retalick ; Loweſtoffe, 32, B. Hallowell ; La Lutine, 32, ———— ; and Sincerity, (cut.)

MALACCA, in the Eaſt Indies, with its dependencies, D : ſurrendered Auguſt 17, 1795, to the Company's forces under Major Browne, in conjunction with the Reſiſtance, 44, E. Paken- ham; and Orpheus, 32, H. Newcombe.

TRINCOMALE, in the Iſland of Ceylon, D : ſurrendered, Auguſt 25, 1795, to the naval and military force under Comm. P. Rainier, and Col. J. Stuart. The Britiſh ſquadron conſiſting of the Suffolk, 74, Comm. P. Rainier ; Centurion, 50, S. Oſborn ; Reſiſtance, 44, E. Pakenham ; Diomede, 44, M. Smith, which was unfortunately loſt in working up into the bay, on her arri- val, Aug. 1 ; (See Britiſh ſhips loſt, &c.) and Heroine, 32, A. H. Gardner ; with 2 Indiamen.

THE COLONY of THE CAPE of GOOD HOPE, D : The Dutch governor having rejected, in the moſt peremptory terms, the propoſals which had been made to him for this ſettlement, to put itſelf under the protection of Great Britain, active hoſtilities were commenced againſt it July 14, 1795, which continued until Sept. 16, when his Majeſty's forces under General A. Clarke, and V.-Adm. the Hon. Sir G. K. Elphinſtone, K. B. obtained on capitulation full poſ- feſſion of the town and colony. The ſquadron, actively employed in this important conqueſt, conſiſted of the Monarch, 74, V. Adm. Elphinſtone ; Capt J. Elphinſtone ; America, 64, Com. J. Blankett ; Stately, 64, B. Douglas ; Echo, (ſloop,) 16, T. Hardy : and Rattleſnake, (ſloop,) 16, J. W. Spranger. In Auguſt, 1796, a ſquadron under the command of R.-Adm. Lucas, of 9 ſhips, was deſtined for the recapture of this ſettlement ; the whole of which were captured, as recorded in the 25th page of this work.

COLOMBO, and its dependencies. in the Iſland of Ceylon, D : ſurrendered, Feb. 15, 1796, to his Majeſty's and the Eaſt-India Company's forces, under the command of Capt. A. H. Gard- ner, and Col. James Stuart. The naval force conſiſte of the Heroine, 32, A. H. Gardner ; Rattleſnake, (ſloop,) 16, E. Ramage ; Echo, (ſloop,) 16, J. Turner ; and ſix of the company's veſſels.

THE ISLANDS of AMBOYNA AND BANDA, in the Eaſt Indies, with their ſeveral de- pendencies, D : ſurrendered to the land and ſea forces commanded by R.-Adm. P. Rainier ; the former on the 16th of Feb. and the latter on the 8th of March, 1796.

THE COLONIES of DEMERARY AND ISSEQUIBO, in the Weſt Indies, D : ſur- rendered without reſiſtance, April 23, 1796, to the forces under Major-General John White, and Comm. Thomas Parr. The ſquadron conſiſting of the Malabar, 54, Comm. T. Parr ;

Scipio,

CAPTURED FROM THE ENEMY 83

Scipio, 64, F. Laforey ; Undaunted, 40, H. Roberts ; La Pique, 40, D. Milne ; and Le Babet, 2c, W. G. Lobb.

THE COLONY of BERBICE, in the West Indies, D : surrendered without resistance, on the same terms as Demerary, &c. and to the same forces, May 2, 1796.

FOUL POINT, on the Island of MADAGASCAR. The French establishment at this place surrendered on capitulation to the Crescent. 36, Capt. J. W. Spranger, accompanied by the Braave, 40, A..Todd, and Sphinx, 20, F. H. Coffin, and was destroyed in January, 1797.

THE ISLAND of TRINIDAD, in the West Indies, S: surrendered on capitulation to the British forces under Lieut.-Gen. Sir R. Abercromby, K. B. and R. Adm. H. Harvey, Feb. 18. The squadron which shared in this conquest consisted of the Prince of Wales, 98, R.-Adm. H. Harvey, Capt. J. Harvey ; Invincible, 74, W. Cayley; Alfred, 74, T. Totty ; Bellona, 74, G. Wilson ; Vengeance, 74, T. M. Russel ; Scipio, 64, C. S. Davers ; Dictator, 64, ——— ; Alarm, 32, E. Fellowes ; Arethusa, 38, T. Wolley ; Favourite, (sloop,) 16, J. A. Wood ; Pelican, (sloop,) 18, ———; Zephyr, (sloop,) 14, R. Laurie ; Terror, (bomb,) 8 ; Thorn, (sloop,) 16, J. Hamstead ; La Victorieuse, 12, E. S. Dickson ; Ulysses, (armed transport,) 44, Lt. G. Lempriere ; Zebra, (sloop,) 19, ———; and Bittern, (sloop,) 16, T. Lavie.

The ISLAND of MINORCA in the Mediterranean, S : taken by the forces under General the Hon. C. Stuart, and Commodore J. T. Duckworth, Nov. 15, 1798 ; the British squadron consisting of the Leviathan, 74, Commodore J. T. Duckworth ; Centaur, 74, J. Markham ; Argo, 44, J. Bowen ; Aurora, 28, H. Digby ; Dolphin, 44, J. Nesbit ; Coromandel, (A. T.) 24, Lieut. R. Simmonds ; Cormorant, 20, Lord M. R. Kerr ; and Constitution, (cutter,) Lieutenant Weston.

The COLONY of SURINAM, D : surrendered, without resistance, to the forces under Lieutenant-General T. Trigge and V.-Admiral Lord H. Seymour, and placed under the protection of his Britannic majesty, August 20, 1799. The ships actively employed upon this service were the Prince of Wales, 98, Vice-Admiral Lord H. Seymour, Captain A. Renon ; Invincible, 74, W. Cayley : Amphitrite, 28, C. Ekins ; Requin, 12, Lieutenant W. W. Senhouse; and four frigates.

The ISLAND of GOREE, on the coast of Africa, F : taken, April 5, 1800, by the Melpomene, 44, Capt. Sir C. Hamilton, accompanied by the Ruby, 64, S. Ferris, and Magnanime, 44, W. Tayler.

The ISLANDS of MALTA and GOZA. These islands, which had recently derived so much importance from the peculiar circumstances of the hostile powers, having been previously taken by the French forces, were put into a state of blockade by the British, on the 26th of September, 1798. Goza surrendered by an honourable capitulation, October 28 following, to Capt. A. J. Ball, of the Alexander, 74, who was then the commanding-officer entrusted with the blockade. Malta, however, held out till the 4th of September, 1800, when it surrendered, after a blockade of nearly two years, to the British forces. The ships which formed the blockade consisted of the Northumberland, 74, G. Martin ; Alexander, 74, A. J. Ball ; Généreux, 74, M. Dixon ; Stately, 64, (armed en flute,) G. Scott ; Charon, 44, (armed en flute,) R. Bridges;

Princess

Princefs Charlotte, 38, T. Stephenfon; Pallas, 38, (armed en flute,) J. Edmonds; Penelope, 36, H. Blackwood; Santa Terefa, 36, R. Campbell; Succefs, 32, S. Peard; Niger, (armed en flute,) 32, J. Hellyer: Champion, 24, Lord W. Stuart; La Bonne Citoyenne, 18, W. Buchanan; Port Mahon, 16, R. Jackfon; El Vincelo, 16, G. Long; Minorca, 16, G. Miller; and Strombolo, (bomb,) 8, A. Thompfon.

The ISLAND of CURACAO, in the Weft Indies, *D :* furrendered, after having claimed the protection of his Britannic Majefty, to the Néréide, 36, Capt. Fr. Watkins, Sept. 12, 1800.

General Statement of Ships captured from the different hoftile Powers, and Ships defiroyed in Action, to the End of the Year 1800.

	Line.		Fifties.		Frigates.		Sloops.		Total.	
	Ships.	Guns.	Ships.	Guns.	Ships.	Guns.	Ships.	Guns.	Ships.	Guns.
French - -	45	3582	2	102	130	4136	143	1666	320	9486
Dutch - -	25	1598	1	50	31	1054	32	346	89	3048
Spanifh - -	8	684	—	—	18	616	49	406	75	1706
Total - - -	78	5864	3	152	179	5806	224	2418	484	14240
Britifh - -	3	222	1	50	11	300	34	438	49	1010
Diff. in favour of Gr. Britain,	75	5642	2	102	168	5506	190	1980	435	13230

PRIVATEERS

Taken or deftroyed, French, 743; Dutch, 15; and Spanifh, 76.—Total, 834.

Befides the above, there have been loft by various accidents, of the enemy's fhips, 10 of the line and nine frigates, with many fmaller veffels;* and, of Britifh fhips, 17 of the line, 2 fifties, 36 frigates, and 48 floops and fmall veffels.

---

* Including the Spanifh fhips San Alexandro, 74, and Rofario, 36. The former wrecked in Palamos-harbour, and the latter in Barcelona-road. Dates unknown to the editor. — We have not included in the above ftatement the French fhips which have been retained by other powers.

Printed by H. L. Galabin, Ingram-Court, Fenchurch-ftreet, London.

For EU product safety concerns, contact us at Calle de José Abascal, 56–1°, 28003 Madrid, Spain or eugpsr@cambridge.org.

www.ingramcontent.com/pod-product-compliance
Ingram Content Group UK Ltd.
Pitfield, Milton Keynes, MK11 3LW, UK
UKHW012336130625
459647UK00009B/329